The *Art* of Starting Over

The *Art* of Starting Over

...And getting it right this time

A Thirty-Day Guide to Creating More Power, Peace, and Pleasure in Your Personal Life

Kiné Corder

iUniverse, Inc.
Bloomington

The Art of Starting Over
A Thirty-Day Guide to Creating More Power,
Peace, and Pleasure in Your Personal Life

iUniverse books may be ordered through booksellers or by contacting:
iUniverse
1663 Liberty Drive
Bloomington, IN 47403
www.iuniverse.com
1-800-Authors (1-800-288-4677)

ISBN: 978-1-4759-4315-3 (sc)
ISBN: 978-1-4759-4314-6 (hc)
ISBN: 978-1-4759-4313-9 (e)

Library of Congress Control Number: 2012914444

Printed in the United States of America

iUniverse rev. date: 8/21/2012

Contents

Preface

A series of events led to the creation of this book. It is made up of life lessons I have learned through my own experiences and the experiences of my friends, colleagues and clients.

I worked as a Barber and Natural Hair stylist for 15 years. During this time I listened to my clients complain about their unhappy lives without doing anything to change. Week after week they would return and I would have to listen to the same complaints. It became frustrating and sad.

To get past my frustration I started offering detailed instructions on what should be done. After trying my suggestions they would return with new stories and this time talked about how much better they felt. This became part of my service and clients began paying for my advice.

I always knew I would write a book, I just never had the right subject. I thought it would be interesting to write about my experience on Extreme Makeover, but somehow it didn't seem like the right book for me. My clients encouraged me to write this book.

Some time passed and after watching the movie "The Pursuit of Happyness" with my sister I decided I would drop everything and take the Series 7 test that I had been avoiding for 10 years. Although I was always good at taking tests I was terrified of taking the Series 7.

After passing the test, I worked as a Financial Advisor for two years with very little income. I could not figure out how someone as caring and smart as I, could not make money in this very lucrative business. I later found out that being a Financial Advisor meant I owned my own business and it would take five years to begin earning the kind of money I was use to.

After reading Chris Gardner's second book "Start Where You Are" I decided I wanted to meet him. One day I drove downtown and walked right up to his front door. Just my luck he was leaving out. I said, "Hi, my name is Kiné and I came to meet you." "Did we have an appointment," he asked. "No, I just finished your book and I wanted to have a ten minute courtesy call like you suggested in the book." He said, "I am leaving out now but go see my assistant and tell her I said to give you twenty minutes."

My appointment was set for a month later. A week later Chris spoke at my church; I waited afterward and asked if I could walk him to his car and pick his brain on the way. He said, "Are you always this aggressive." I answered, "Yeah I am it's the only way I know how to get what I want." He laughed and we talked for a few minutes and I had my courtesy call the next month.

Six months later I decided to start over; for the second time.. I did it once when I became the spokesperson for ABC's Extreme Makeover and now I was doing it again. At first most people thought I was crazy but I knew that it was out of sanity that I decided to make a change. Then people started admiring the will I had to start fresh with statements like, "you are so brave", "you are so smart", "you are so powerful"; I wasn't trying to be any of those things, I was just pursuing happiness.

That is when I realized what my book would be about. I would show people exactly how I lived. I would help them understand how to make decisions that would help them reach their goals and how to be happier than they are now. I had done it a few times and each time it got easier because I had a better plan. Because I seek the maximum pleasure out of life, I will not let anything stand in my way of being happy not even me.

Dedication

This book is dedicated to my family.

Mommy, I love, adore and honor you more than words can say. You are the reason for every good thing I have ever done. In my eyes you are perfect. Thank you for encouraging every creative thought. Dad, thanks for always keeping your word to me and showing me how a man should treat a lady. You always let me be myself and live out my dreams.

Thank you to the best big sister a girl could ask for. You are my biggest fan. Thanks for showing this nerd how to look like a cool girl. Little sister, we had a tight bond from day one. Thank you for admiring me and inspiring me at the same time. Brother, you taught me a valuable life lesson that I wish I would have learned earlier. Keep working hard.

To my nephew I say thanks for filling the void. I've been learning from you since you were born. To my younger nieces and nephew, thank you for showing me my reflection. (Play) daughter, thank you for calling me mom and showing me what I was capable of.

Granny, I miss you dearly but your words of wisdom are in this book and inside of me. Thank you for being such a lady. You were a great example.

Acknowledgements

There is no better friend in the world than my best friend. I could write a whole book of thank yous and that wouldn't be enough. You got excited with me every time I tried something new. For that I am eternally grateful.

Thank you Papa for helping me understand when to be emotional and when to be logical; and most important when to be powerful and when to be gentle.

Thank you uncle (and other father), for financial and mental support; also, for making me laugh all the time.

Matti & Kevin Williams, thank you for believing in me. I cherish the blessing you gave me that made this book possible. You will always be part of the Presidential family.

Thank you, Secret Squirrel for building my self-esteem and reminding me that I had a magic wand. You stuck in there with me and my crazy dreams.

Thank you, Step-daughters for making my heart bigger. I am not sure if I knew love until I loved you (and I still do).

A big thank you goes to Kelly Koehler, Mark Mueller, Chevez Frazier, Moneca Reid and all my former and current friends. You have all made me who I am today.

Lastly, thank you to my editors; Felicia Peoples your encouragement kept me going. Aja Williams, your calm spirit is what makes you good at what you do. It was great working with you. I can't wait for the next one.

Thank you, God for giving me the knowledge, experiences and creativity to write and publish this book. Oh yeah and the money. It was not easy but it was worth it.

Author's Instructions

This book is a thirty day step by step guide to starting your life over. You can read it and complete each exercise in thirty days or you can take your time, extending it to ninety days, six months or a year. It is up to you. I challenge you however to do the opposite of what you normally do. If you normally speed through everything, work at a slower pace. If you usually procrastinate, give yourself a deadline for completing an exercise.

I started this book with the idea "Ready, Set, Go!" in mind. True winners don't just go; they train first, they focus and then they take off. When you watch a track meet you will hear, "runners take your marks," "get set" and then "go" or the gun goes off. We can use this same approach in life. Why can't we do exactly what they are doing during each one of those stages? This is all part of the race.

I ran track when I was in grade school and high school and my coach broke it down to us this way: "When you hear runners take your marks, you stand in the spot that has been assigned to you. While you are there, you should evaluate the situation. You are already trained and everything you need is inside of you. Now reach down and pull out what you need. You look at the path you are going to run. You look at the obstacles in your way. Do you see the sun shining too brightly? Is there a rock in your lane? Look at the way your lane curves and decide how much speed you need to have when you hit that curve. Ask yourself what it will take to win this race. Commit to finishing, winning and doing your best. You should also take this time to loosen up. Shake your muscles out. Release the tension in your jaws, neck, shoulders, hips and legs. Shake off any fear you have because this is it. You are going to win this race."

That is the "taking your mark" in a track meet. You can apply those same principles to life. When you are setting a goal or making a change or going for something you really want, you have to take your mark. See where you are starting and where the finish line is. If you cannot see the finish line from where you are standing, visualize it. You have practiced and trained for this moment. Now it is time to put all your training into action. Look at the obstacles in your way and plot a course around them or over them or right through them. Figure out when you need to pick up speed or when you may need to slow down. Look at your opponents so that you know what you are up against. They shouldn't scare you because you have practiced, prepared and trained for this event. "Take your mark, runner!"

Next the runner will hear "get set" or "ready." Coach Mueller says when you hear this, you need to get in your position to push off past the opponent. The runner who gets the best start wins. You want a fast start to build up momentum. In training you learned the best position. You learned where your hands should be; down to each finger tip. You know how your head should be held. You know where your feet should dig into the track. You get your legs spread the perfect distance apart to give you the best start. You are ready. Your head is down. You are no longer looking at the track; you made your evaluation and you are now listening for the "go." There is no other sound. The voices in your head are quiet and the crowd is a whisper. The wind is still and you are at attention. You are not tense.

That is the "get set" or "ready" in a track meet. In life once you have trained and taken your mark, you need to get ready to go. You need to make sure you have put all the things in place that will get you to your goal. You want to make sure you are going to have a good start. You need to stand correctly, look the part, dress the part and position yourself to win the race. At this point you are no longer plotting your course. You are no longer evaluating or checking for obstacles. Your head is down. You are listening for the sound; the sound of opportunity knocking. You do not hear your friends, family or co-workers. All you hear is the whisper of the still small voice inside of you. You feel yourself breathing slowly, deeply and your heart is beating calmly. You have no fear. You are waiting. You are not tense or afraid. You are at attention. You are set and ready!

The last part of starting in a track meet is the most important part. I talked a little about it in "get set." Coaches Mueller and Koehler both said the runner with the best start wins. You have to put everything into the start so that you get in front of the competition and have enough momentum to push through the hurdles and not get weighed down by the drag. When the runners hear go, they blast off like they are the only people in the world. They know they have everything to lose and everything to gain. The runner wants to win. The sound "go" is the sweetest sound ever. They have been waiting for this moment. They trained for this moment. It is time. Runners run every race as if it is the only race and there may not be another one.

Life principle "Go" brings us to the good part and the hard part in life. Many people can take their mark and get ready, but few people actually ever go. When you go, you set yourself apart from the lazy, the tired and the fearful. You prove yourself to be one of the world's finest. When you win, and only you know when that is, you prove to yourself that you are the best. Train, focus, position and "GO!"

I want you to center on the idea that you must "take your mark," "get ready" and "go." The first part of this book is about your training and focus. You have some training in life that will get you through your endeavor. You have gone to school, had some life experiences, observed the experiences of others, or maybe you have had some failures. Whatever your method of training, you have put in some work and it counts. So what does it count toward? It helps you prepare for the race. Use your training to get ready for whatever life will bring. Build up your decision making muscles. Stretch out so you see how flexible you are. Push yourself so you know what you can handle and how strong you are. Correct your mistakes and learn from the best.

The second part of the book is to get you on your mark. You can't start from anywhere. You have to get on your mark so that each step you make counts. Wherever you are right now, you need to train so that you will be invited to the mark, know where the mark is, and know what to do when you get there. Runners, take your mark. Once you have trained to the fullest and found your mark, get set.

The third part of the book is to get you set. You need to strategize, make a plan and be prepared for what will come. Training is only half the battle.

This part of the book gets you focused. It reminds you that you are the one doing the running but you have a support system and cheer squad. Let this book be your coach. Together we will make sure you are prepared mentally, physically, emotionally and spiritually. Come back to this book whenever you need to. It will get you back on track. Read as many books as you like but know that this is the book that you can take throughout life as a handbook for success. While you were reading and writing your answers you were being coached building your confidence. This is your road map, your step by step guide and your new best friend. You are not alone.

This book is about taking your mark and getting set. Rest periods and rewards are factored in to the program so do not worry about getting worn out. The "GO" is the rest of your life. You will take your mark and get set many times in life. Know when it is time to "GO."

Whether you were forced to start over because of a job loss or a divorce, or if you decided to start over with a with a new business venture, this book will become your handbook and blue print. Do each exercise and discover what's missing in your life. By the end of this book you will be clear on what you desire and know how to create a life full of those desires.

Let's get started...

Day 1 – Commitment

This book is useless unless you make a commitment to indulge in the exercises, put your all into it and make a commitment to yourself to do what makes you happy. If this is a time in your life when you are either making a choice to start over or you are forced to start over, take the time to get it right. If you have the opportunity now to start over you may as well do something that makes you happy.

In order to reach your goals, be happy, and really make a change, you have to make a commitment to do the things suggested in the chapters. You have to be honest with yourself and be persistent until you get what you want. Can you do that?

If so, I want you to make a commitment right now before you read any further. You have to write the commitment for yourself because it is not for me; it is for you. It is important that you write it in your own words in your own language and in a way that you know what you are committing to.

Below is a short commitment form that you can use to get started or you can write your own using this as a guide.

I, _____ commit and promise myself to take the necessary steps to make a change in my life. I understand that starting over takes dedication and courage. I am both dedicated and courageous. I am capable of reaching my goals and I will begin the journey today. I will put forth my best effort.

This commitment is of sound mind and not a fly by night emotional decision. It is well thought out and I have considered all the possibilities. I understand that it will take time and that it is a process. I intend to enjoy that process and learn as I go through it. I also promise to share my knowledge so that someone else can succeed the way I have.

I am committed. _____ *(initial)*

Sign: _____

Date: _____

The elements of the commitment letter:

1. Your name
2. A statement of what you are committing to.
3. State your dedication.
4. Initial, sign and date the commitment.

After you write your letter of commitment, put it in a place where you can see it daily. When you see it, it will serve as a reminder to you and assist you in keeping your commitment.

Day 2 – Questionnaire

Do I know my life's purpose?

Yes   No

Am I living that purpose?

Yes   No

Is my daily activity in line with my life's purpose?

Yes   No

If you answered *YES* to all of the above questions, this book will be a refresher course for you. If you answered *NO* to any of the above questions you should go forward to finally find your purpose and start living the life you deserve and desire. You made a commitment so these questions are not to set you back but to identify where you are starting. Wherever you are is ok.

I have to make some serious changes in my life?

Yes   No

I am committed to making those changes?

Yes   No

I would like to live my life with a purpose?

Yes   No

If you answered *NO* to any of the above questions you need to ask yourself if you are being honest. If you bought this book or if someone gave you this book, deep down inside you want to make a commitment in making a change to live your life with a purpose. Give it some thought and decide if now is the right time. If it is not, you can either read the book anyway or put it down and come back when you are ready.

If you said *YES* to change then you are in the right place. I am proud to be a part of your next stage in life and I am here with you. I will not be there in person everyday but if you need to talk you can schedule a consultation by sending an email to consultation@kinecorder.com. Even though I will not always be there physically, I am there mentally and spiritually. (For those of you who are not spiritual, don't worry I won't get "holier than thou" on you.)

I want you to know that someone is there because I remember going through some changes by myself and wishing someone was there. Someone who could say, "everything is ok;" someone who could hold my hand or push me when I was weak. You are not alone. So get ready to find what you are looking for.

By now you should have written and signed your commitment. Be sure to keep it where you can see it. Below are a few more questions that need to be answered in order to help you realize what things you need to change and what things you should keep the same.

Do I usually do what people want me to do instead of what I want to do?

Yes   No

Do I put off until tomorrow what I can do today?

Yes   No

Am I afraid to pursue my dreams?

Yes   No

By answering *NO* to all of these questions you are clear what you want, need and are capable of. If you answered *YES* to any of them, you are still ok because you are obviously ready to conquer your fear. Brave is feeling the fear and doing it anyway. You can do whatever you set your mind and heart to do. You don't have to take away all the fear but you do have to push through it. Eventually as you become more confident in your decision, you will not feel the fear anymore and you will be able to answer *NO* to all three questions.

I know where I go wrong?

Yes   No

If so, describe where you feel you go wrong. You can use an example of a past experience. Feel free to be as descriptive as possible.

_____
_____
_____
_____

I know what people think of me?

Yes   No

How does it make you feel?

_____
_____

_____

_____

_____

_____

_____

_____

Am I aware of the challenges that keep me from accomplishing my dreams?

Yes   No

If so, what are they? If you do not know right now come back and write them down when you do.

_____

_____

_____

_____

_____

_____

_____

I prioritize my activities and make the best of my time.

Yes   No

The answer to this question is important. If you answered *YES*, some of the task before you will be easier. If you answered *NO*, you will build the habit of prioritizing and being accountable for your daily activity while reading the book.

Call to action:
   1.   Answer the commitment questions above.

Day 3 – Self-Evaluation

Self-evaluation is a process where you look inside yourself and ask, "Who have I become?" Is this who I want to be and if not what am I missing? What makes me happy? Do I have enough of it in my life and if not, why? Self-evaluation can be painful and scary the first time you do it. If you are ready to change than you have to do it now. It will feel good to really know what you want, why you want it and how to get it.

Self-evaluation is the process of finding out what you desire. That means finding out who you want to be and what kind of life you want to live. It means discovering what moves you. It allows you to acknowledge some bad habits and idiosyncrasies.

First, ask yourself "who am I?" Am I selfish? Am I a push over? Am I evil? Am I a nice person? Chances are you will found you have more than one personality. At times you are nice and at times you are not. At times you are lazy and at times you are not. There will be a pattern though. You will see consistency in some areas and be able to judge who you have become. You will see yourself being lazy too often. You can take this to mean that there is something there that you are afraid of or that does not interest you. When you see a pattern you can make an assessment of that behavior.

Think about your actions and watch yourself. Take note of your habits. Take note of your feelings. Figure out when you are hurt, happy, lazy, vulnerable, strong or passive. Make sure you are evaluating the people involved and note how they change your perception or your actions. You should also become aware of what gets you moving and the people who bring you down and those that motivate you. You will learn what inspires you and what makes you fall in love at first sight. You will also see what makes you want to run and hide. When these things are revealed, you are learning who you are. You are evaluating yourself.

Next, you have to decide if that is who you want to be. Are you happy with the decisions you have made? Are you satisfied with your way of making decisions? Do you treat people the way you want to be treated? Do you demand that people treat you the way you deserve to be treated? Do you like yourself? Do others like you? Do you like other people? What about you do people love? Is that the same thing you love about yourself? What or who makes you do the things you do? Are you spiritual or religious? Do you have common sense, book smarts or street smarts? Are you business savvy? Who are you?

Self-evaluation is the beginning of the process. What is the sense in evaluating yourself if you are not going to do anything about it? You are making these evaluations so that you can determine where to go from here. The next step is to figure out who you want to be and commit to becoming that person. It is your life to change and start over as often as you like. Just don't hurt yourself and don't hurt anyone else.

Write down who you want to be. Then say it out loud and mean it. When you get off course get back on. Find people that can help you keep your commitment and hold you accountable. Make a plan and stick to it but be realistic. Adjust it as needed and check back to see what accomplishments you have made. When you find that you are there, celebrate, reward yourself and keep going.

Do it now. Put it on paper and read it out loud. Say I am going to be......
and make a list of all the things you want to be as a person. Write everything from every aspect; emotional, physical, mental, and spiritual.

Let me give you an example. There once was a girl who lived in a small town in New York State. She always felt too big for the town she lived in and she knew that one day she would have to leave. Well, as she grew older, fear of the big city began to set in. When she would speak of her dream to go to the city people would tell her it was a bad idea. They would give her all the reasons she should not go. She had an opportunity to study abroad in France when she was in college but she heard something on the news about Europe and decide that maybe that wasn't for her. A few years later she got another opportunity to transfer to Chicago to start a new branch for her company. She heard stories about how lonely the big city could be and how dangerous it was so she turned it down. The girl began to think that maybe she wasn't too big for this small town after all. Maybe this is as good as it gets. "This is comfortable and it has worked so why change it," her friends and family would say. She responded to herself, "because I'm not happy here." Out loud she just nodded her head and agreed but inside she longed for change.

One day she looked up and everything she dreamed about was a faded memory. No husband, no children, no big job in the city. No great travel stories, no trophies or plaques. Just an ordinary life that would not be so bad if it was the life she really wanted. "Is this really as good as it gets or is there more?" "Did I miss my chance?", she asked herself. "No," she answered. "It's never too late." I am going to start today. "I put my hand to God that I will not stop until my dreams come true."

I will become more spiritual. I won't just go to church on Sunday. I will live a life rooted in peace and love and faith in all that I am capable of and all that the world is capable of. I will stop letting people lead me places I don't want to go. I will stop being passive and start telling people how I really feel. I will stop being evil to my friends and family. I know that I am only doing it because I am hurting inside. I will express myself kindly and honestly and I will feel good when I do it. I will start eating better and taking walks to the park. I will start going to the next town over to meet new people and I will actually go to New York City so I will know what it is really like.

Later that year the young lady took her first trip to New York City. She shopped, ate and saw a show. She took a taxi and the train. She even rented a car and drove around. She honked her horn and yelled at other drivers. She found the neighborhood she thought she would like to live in and she met a few people at a wine store. She surprised herself and had a little summer fling. One afternoon before she was to leave New York, she set at an outdoor café and began to write her plan. She mouthed the words under her breath, "Things are going to start happening for me today." I am going to be a successful person. I will feel successful because I will live the life I choose for myself. She found after planning, that it would realistically take her two years to save up enough money and get herself mentally ready to move. She did it.

She saved religiously and she prayed for strength. She started being honest with herself and the people around her. She didn't always tell them what she was thinking because she knew not everyone would share her vision and she did not want to try to teach them. She would much rather let them learn from her example; from her actions. Talking is cheap she discovered and thinking is even cheaper unless you decide to turn it into a real plan. But even the plan isn't enough if you do not work it.

She was following her plan. She put in for a transfer at her job and a few months later she got it. 2 ½ years went by so fast because she made a commitment and she stuck with it. "New York City, here I come," she said. After working for the company for another year, she moved to a bigger company where she could advance and married her next door neighbor a year after that. It was the funniest story. They still own both houses and rent one out. What a life.

When asked what she learned, she answered, "Success is when what you want to do becomes what you have done." It's not something that happens over night and it does not have to be fancy." "You can make the decision to go for it in one night and once you make that commitment stick to it for life." It will happen because you will make it happen and you won't stop until it does.

This girl's life was changed because she made a decision, stuck with it and saw it through. She finally believed she deserved it. You can do this same thing in your life; it all starts with a little evaluation. Go back to the questionnaire page and look at the answers to those questions. This will give you a good start to evaluate yourself. Remember to evaluate yourself mentally, emotionally, physically and spiritually.

Decide who you want to be in each of the four areas and then take a look back at yourself and see if this is who you are. If not, write down the things about yourself that keep you from being that person.

Call to action:
1. Evaluate yourself
2. Write down who you want to be
3. Make a decision to become that person

Day 4 – Giver or Taker

Are you a giver or a taker? What does that mean and why does that matter? This is something you may have discovered in your self-evaluation or maybe it is something you never really thought about.

In life generally people are either givers or takers. Of course there have been times when you have been both but most people lean toward one side or the other. You may have a knack at getting what you want without even asking for it. You may be the type of person that helps people before they even realize they need help. You may get offers, free stuff and assistance with little to no effort. You may feed the hungry, cure the sick or grant wishes like Santa Claus. When you were giving, did you expect something in return or were the smiles on the faces enough for you? When you were receiving did you ever think how you could repay the favor or what you could do in return?

The answers to those questions will determine in part whether you are a giver or a taker. If you like to receive so much that you rarely get around to figuring out how to give back, you may be a taker. That's not necessarily a bad thing; just an observation. If you are so busy giving that you rarely stop to think about how you will be compensated, then you may be a giver. Again, not a bad thing; just an observation.

You can think about where you fall while you read this short story called "Where is mine, do I have yours?"

On a country road where everything seems to belong to the Gods, a couple of animals began to gather. They noticed that all of the humans had left the town. They could not decide if this was a good thing or a bad thing. What they did realize is that the humans played a role in their survival and without them there, everyone would have to do their part to keep the place going. There was a cow, a chicken, a horse, a dog and a bird.

The team had decided that the cow would provide milk, the chicken would give eggs, the horse would plow the garden, the bird would water everything and the dog would manage. Dog slept most of the day because he did not have a job until night time. Every night when it was time for dinner, dog would set the table and be the first one there waiting to eat. Cow would provide milk for breakfast every morning and make orange juice or lemonade for dinner using the fruit she collected underneath the trees in the front yard.

Horse would plow and pick the vegetables from the garden for dinner and would get the apples off the trees for breakfast. He was the tallest and the strongest so he did not mind doing the work. Chicken had enough eggs every morning to go with the apples and milk that Cow and Horse had provided.

Bird was always up early and she went to bed early too. She hung out with her friends most of the day but she was always home in time to eat dinner. She did not really know what to bring or how she could help but she did bring all the dishes to the kitchen for chicken to wash. Bird was the youngest and the others took good care of her.

Horse loved Dog. They had been best friends for many years and had seen each other through many different struggles. Usually Horse was listening to Dog's problems and coming through when Dog needed a helping hand, but it was okay because Horse always had his back. Horse made good decisions and was pretty proud of that. Dog did not think much about making decisions. In fact, he barely made them at all. He felt like life would handle itself.

Cow and Chicken were good friends too. They were about the same age and they often watched after each other's children. When Cow's husband, died Chicken spent several nights with her cleaning up and entertaining the children. When Chicken's mother came to town, Cow was there to make sure that everything went smoothly.

Everything was going fine until the humans came back to town just as mysteriously as they had left. They all started to forget their bond and they went back to their old jobs working for the humans. Papa Human worked in the field and took care of the animals. Momma Human did her best to help Papa Human. Little Human stayed in her bedroom reading most of the time. She was an "A" student and reading was her favorite past time. She came out to help her parents when she was called upon. Together the animals and the humans took care of each other and they took what they needed from each other.

In a perfect world we would all take our fair share and give what we had to offer. We would never take too much and never give too much. We would give what we could and take what we needed. Usually greed takes hold of people and they begin a pattern of taking. They eat dinner without bringing anything or without setting the table or doing the dishes. This is a Taker. The Givers catch the food, cook and clean up afterward without expecting the Takers to do anything. They do not even ask the Takers to contribute.

I know you were probably expecting the story to be more cut and dry like my explanation of givers and takers so that you could easily point out who the givers were and who the takers were. In life it may not be that plain and simple. You may be a giver who looks like a taker. For instance the little human in the story seemed like a taker. All she did all day was lie in her room and read. She did not help out unless she was asked. However, her parents may think of her as a giver. She gets good grades and she gives them what they ask of her. It is exciting for them to discuss their daughter who reads and gets all A's. That may be all they need from her and she provides that. On the other hand, if her parents expected her to help out around the house, do chores and run errands, then she is not living up to their expectations and she seems like a taker.

When you are evaluating yourself and deciding if you are a giver or taker, you have to look at the expectation. Some expectations are social and others are personal. Your friends, family and colleagues have an expectation of you. They expect you to do certain things. When you do not live up to their expectations, they may feel as if you are not doing your fair share. Socially there are things that are expected of you because you are a woman or wife, parent or doctor, or whatever title you fall under. With each title comes an expectation. Check to see if you are living up to your part of the bargain.

Who are you: a giver or a taker? Do you come to dinner empty handed and leave before it is time to clean up? Do you invite people out to eat or over for dinner without expecting them do anything in return? Do you ask to borrow money that you never pay back or are you never in a position to lend anyone anything? Ask yourself, do I take more than I give? Or ask yourself do I give more than I take? When you are part of an organization do you pay your dues, do you commit your time and energy and do you show up when asked? Write down the answers to some of the above questions. When you are finished make an assessment.

Write an X next to which one you lean toward.

_____ Giver _____ Taker

Are you okay with that? If others see you this way, is that who you want to be? If so, then are you clear on what that means? If you are a Giver you can tire out at some point and resent the people who take from you. Know that if you are a Taker it could run out at some point and people can become frustrated with you. When that happens you will have to start giving and you will not be able to take again until everyone around you feels some reciprocity. What most takers do when the well runs dry is go find a new well. And what most givers do when they resent their takers is go find some new takers to give to so they can feel good about it again. You are who you are. I am not saying either way is good or bad. The world is made up of givers and takers. You have to know what you are so you can adjust as needed.

You should always think about how to get what you need to live and survive. However, you should also think about how the people around you will live and survive. I call that "where is mine, do I have yours?" This is when you are willing to work for what you want but are not so attached to it that you would not share it with your neighbor.

Call to action:

1. Make a list of people who owe you and what they owe you.
2. Decide if you want something in return and what.
3. Make a list of people you owe and what you owe them.
4. Decide what you are willing to give back and when you will give it.

Day 5 – Who do you admire?

Today you will give some thought to who has lived a life you could see yourself living. You will also consider who has been the type of person you would like to be or would like to be around. Think about who gets your attention with their attitude, accomplishments and contributions. You may already know or you may have to give it some thought. Let your mind run free.

This was difficult for me because I was taught to look inside myself for inspiration. I was taught to rely on my own strengths and to compete only with myself. Now it is okay for me to rely on myself but it is also okay for me to admire someone who has gone before me.

What does it mean to admire someone? I found these definitions: have a high regard and esteem for, approve of, like, be in awe of. The last one was the one that struck me the most. There are many people that I like, think highly of or have esteem for. But there were not many people that I would actually say I was in awe of. With careful consideration I found that there were a few people I admired. There were different things about these people that I admired. There was someone in entertainment, business, high society, and civil rights.

Who are you in awe of? Who would leave you speechless if they walked in the room right now? Think about who would still have your attention an hour after they were out of your presence. Ok now take away the person you lust after. Think about the person you would buy a ticket to hear speak because you plan to do whatever they suggest. Think about the person who you would quit your job and become their personal assistant gratuitously. No, you do not get to sleep with them. You get to work for them, get their advice, and watch how they live in real life on a daily basis. You do not get to share their clothes and they are not going to take care of you. You are still going to be you, only you will now be the assistant to the man or woman who is doing it the way you want to do it.

Who is that person?
(Write down up to 3 people)

1.
2.
3.

It is okay to admire more than one person. You may have different reasons for admiring different people. You may have one you admire for their business acumen, one for their personal character and one for their philanthropic spirit. Whatever the reason, it is okay. Why do you like that particular person? Do they have something you would like to have more of? What would you do with it if you had it?

It is my advice that at least one of the people on your list be someone you can get in touch with. If you are like me, you will do whatever it takes to get in touch with the person you admire and ask (beg) them to mentor or communicate with you.

You would be surprised to know that most people want to pass on their knowledge. Most people are honored when they find out that you admire them. They are usually more than willing to discuss how they did it and give out advice. What you are up against is time. They may be busy and not have the time to give you the attention you deserve. But be patient and stick in there. Let them know that you are ready when they are. If you stop trying, maybe that was not the right person for you. That's what I did and still have to do with my mentors.

To find my three mentors, I waited a year for one and 5 months for another. It did not matter to me because they were worth the wait. The third one was my mother and she is always available whenever I need her and always cheerful about whatever I ask. That is what I admire about her. She is a lady in every sense of the word. I practice being lady like: mild and soft.

My mother is a lioness; she is strong beyond measure but she knows when to be weak. I have this saying about her: "she will never beat you, but she will always win." I guess she learned it from her mother, my grandmother, who is so lady like that she can make a curse word sound sweet.

It is my advice and experience that you want to be mentored by someone who has done what you are want to do. This way they can tell you what the journey is like. They can help you by advising you through the mistakes they have made and give you encouragement. Do not get too tied up in the person and what they do or have not done. It is still your dream and with or without them, you have to make it happen.

It can be disappointing if the mentor you choose does not want to be a mentor or if they do not live up to the idea you had of them. I hope that does not happen to you however, it is possible. My mentor, Chris Gardner tells a story about how he was reaching out to people to get advice and direction and they were too busy or too mean to share their experience with him.

When I was choosing my mentors, I wanted a female in business, a male in business and someone very close to me. I chose my mother because she has the spirit and personality I want to have personally. I chose the other two because they had the business accomplishments as well as the attitude I wanted. I needed a mentor who, at the core, was already like me; kind, loving, honest and loyal. I wanted to see how they took those characteristics that in business can be seen as weaknesses, and used them to their advantage. Being kind does not make you a wimp. Quite the contrary, being kind lets others know how you expect to be treated. I wanted mentors who were strong in their business lives and loving in their personal lives. I wanted someone who had made an impression on the world but was not considered famous. I just thought about who moved me, captured my attention and had done amazing things in their industry. I knew that the universe would reveal them to me and put me in a situation to meet them. I found my mentors by doing the things I normally do like reading, working and writing. I found one at his office in downtown Chicago. The other I found by working on a cruise with an old friend of mine. When the moment was right, I presented myself to each of them and they accepted my invitation. I have always been told, ask and you shall receive.

Did you list 1-3 people that you admire? If you have not already, take some time now to do so. If you think you need more time, take as much as you need. The reason I suggest this is because this book is made for you to do certain things within a certain timeline. Getting them all done will ensure your success. Additionally, having a clear understanding of who you admire will assist you in other areas of the work we are going to do. Finally, it will probably be easier than you think if you just search inside yourself and pay attention to what is important to you. You do not have to pick the mentors the same way I did, but you do have to find someone who makes you feel powerful. I want you to make sure that your "admiree" is someone you can stick with through your journey as you start this new endeavor and live it. Remember you can be inspired by anyone but your "admiree" has a deeper meaning to you.

Now that you have figured out who you admire, I want you to write down the things you like about them. Whether it is a strength you have or wish you had, write it down. Also write down why you like it. They may have 3 or 4 strengths you like. It is up to you how many you want to write down. Use the space below to write. If you need more space, write it on another sheet of paper.

Name(s): (*Example: Chris Gardner*)

_____

Strength or accomplishment: (*business savvy, owns his own company and is a published author*)

_____

Reason: (*Published books, speaks publicly, built a million dollar company.*)

_____
_____
_____
_____

Name(s):

_____

Strength or accomplishment:

_____

Reason:

_____
_____
_____
_____

Name(s):

_____

Strength or accomplishment:

_____

Reason:

_____
_____
_____
_____

Now that you have listed the strengths and accomplishments that you would like to emulate and the reason behind it, you can begin living it. It feels good to know that you are not the only one out there. It feels good to know there is a standard and you have something to reach for. It is motivating to have something to live up to and someone to look up to. If you do not get to meet your mentor face to face, then begin paying attention to their life however you can.

Read over your list and utilize it later when you are discovering your purpose in life and when you are setting your goals. If you do not already know your "would be" mentors personally, you need to set a goal to meet them. You need to ask them if they will be your mentor and know what you need from them. Would you like to meet them once a month or twice a year? Before you go to them, be ready for them to ask you those questions. Do not make them feel uncomfortable but let them know you are serious. Offer to give them something in return. Chances are they have most of their needs filled but offer anyway. If you get a meeting with them, be thankful and thoughtful and bring a gift. Everyone loves a gift and it shows that you understand and appreciate that they are doing this out of the kindness of their hearts. Also, don't lose them because you are too pushy, impatient or inconsiderate. Think positive and you will get the mentor you deserve; one who will help you in whatever way he or she can.

Call to action:
1. Choose a mentor (1-3)
2. Make a list of their strengths and accomplishments that you admire most.
3. Write why you admire those strengths and begin emulating them in your life.
4. If you do not already know them attempt to meet them.
5. Ask if they would be willing to mentor you.
6. Set periodic meetings with your mentor to hold you accountable.

Day 6 – Accomplishments

I have a nephew who is 15 years younger than I am. He is one of my best friends. Of course, we still maintain a certain level of auntie respect but we can really let our hair down when it is just us. Sometimes when he is down, he will come and talk to me and I try my best to give him advice that starts from who he is; not advice based on who I want him to be. Often times as parents, mentors and loved ones, we see the potential and then give advice based on who we want the person to become rather than who they are right now. We have to give advice that they can understand and implement. More importantly, when giving advice I have learned to listen more than talk because oftentimes people do not want advice as much as they want to vent. If you let them talk long enough, sometimes they discover the answer for themselves. The next time someone asks you for advice or you ask someone else, see what happens when listening is the basis of the conversation.

One day when I was about 24, I was fed up with my life. I was complaining because I felt like I was taking two steps back and not getting anywhere. I have always been a go getter so when things are not going my way I would get really hard on myself. I would start blaming myself with things like maybe I am not working hard enough or maybe I missed the opportunity. One day I was mentally drained and I asked my 9 year old nephew to go for a walk with me. Little did I know it would end with a nine year old giving me advice. I guess it is like they say, "out of the mouths of babes." So as I am telling him what I am feeling and how tired of waiting I am, he is just listening quietly. I continued to complain and fuss about how I needed change and how I was ready for my big break and how I only had one more year to do all the great things I had imagined I would do by age 26. All I knew was that I had big dreams and they were taking too long to come along.

As my nephew listened to me complain, he decided to say something. He began by saying, "Auntie." I stopped talking and he went on to say, "You know what I noticed? You always talk about what you want to do but you never talk about what you have already done. You have done a lot and I never hear you talk about that. I always hear other people say how great you are but I never really hear you say how great you are."

I was speechless. One, I knew he was smart but that was one of the smartest statements I had ever heard… period. Not just from a nine year old but from any person. Two, I was speechless because he was right. I did not talk about my accomplishments. Once I accomplished it, I would move on to the next goal. I did not take time out to celebrate or remember my hard work or to thank or reward myself. I would just move on to the next thing.

"Wow," I said. "You're right." I did not complain the rest of the night. We started talking about something else and I thanked him not only for being a good listener but for being honest enough to tell me exactly what I needed to hear. That night I got home and I began making a list of my accomplishments. It was not easy at first. I had blocked some things out; I had over looked others. I had to be proud enough to consider other things as accomplishments.

From that day to this day, I do not stop thinking about my accomplishments. I make a mental note of them and I thank myself for getting it done. When I hear myself complain, I stop and think about that day with my nephew. I say to myself, "you have done great things and you will do more great things in due time." I thank my nephew for that advice often and I pass it on every chance I get.

Do not let your life pass you by while you focus on the wrong things. Enjoy your accomplishments. What have you done that you feel added value to your life? Did you graduate from any schools? Did you write any papers or articles that got published? Did you win any awards or trophies or certificates? How did that make you feel? How long did the feeling last? Maybe it was something as small as getting the courage to go and talk to the girl you had a crush on. Maybe you planned an event at your church that went well. Or maybe it was big like you were president of an organization or you invented something. However big or small, it may seem to the world that it does not matter, but what matters is how it made you feel. I will tell you one of my biggest accomplishments and when you read it you may think, "who cares?" But for me it was life changing and everlasting. It is an accomplishment that I remember when I need some moral boosting or extra self-esteem,. An accomplishment doesn't mean other people rewarded you or noticed your work. It means you were proud of yourself.

I worked in the hair care industry for many years before I started my life over and became a Financial Advisor. I had seen many clients in both industries and they tell you their life stories. I love listening to people talk about their lives. One day a few days after Halloween, I was at work when a little boy about 9 or 10 years old named Christopher walked in with his mother to get a haircut. I was new to the barber shop so I never met Christopher before. His mother told me what haircut he wanted and she walked away. Before sitting down, she mentioned that Christopher was very talkative and that I did not have to listen to him if I did not want to. Most kids are talkative but adults have usually trained them to stop talking. I like when children are able to express themselves so if he wanted to talk it would not bother me.

As I began cutting Christopher's hair, he began to speak. I noticed that he stuttered and that it took him a long time to get through his stories. Now I am patient so I can listen, but I often feel bad for people that stutter because it looks like it hurts them. I was willing to wait for him but I could tell that he was not being patient with himself. Christopher was very excited about his vampire costume that he wore on Halloween. I could tell it was important for him to describe it to me. He tried to tell me about his black cape, his suit and fangs with blood on them but he just could not get it all out. His brain was moving faster than his mouth.

Somehow I knew that Christopher thought that if he did not hurry up and tell me, I, or his mother was going to tell him to shut up. This pressure was making him more nervous so his stuttering got worse. Just then, exactly what Christopher was afraid of happened. His mother says, "Hush and let the lady cut your hair. Girl, don't feel like you have to listen to him. I always tell him to hurry up and tell me the story or just forget it." Now I am sure this woman loved her son and had no idea that she was making him afraid to talk. She was just being human and did not realize that she had the power to help him stop stuttering.

I told the woman it was okay. "I am his until I finish his hair cut so he can talk as long as he likes." I turned the clippers off, turned the barber chair around and told Christopher, "look at me," and he did. I continued, "Every word you have to say is important to me. I want to hear about your Halloween costume. I want you to stop, think about what you want to say and take your time and tell me all about it. I am listening." Christopher closed his eyes, opened them back up and started speaking **clearly**. He told me everything; slowly, without one stuttering word. He described his costume, the party, the prize he won and all the candy he collected.

I could not believe my ears. I wanted to cry, but I kept my composure so that Christopher would not be scared. I was so happy and proud of him. I think his mother wanted to cry too. When I finished his haircut, she came over to pay me and looked me in my eyes and said thank you so much. "Christopher has stuttered all his life. I have never seen him speak like that." Christopher on the other hand was not moved. He just kept speaking slowly and telling me how he liked his haircut and how he thought the kids at school would like it too. It was incredible to us but just an average day to young Christopher.

After they left the barbershop, the owner asked me how I did that. I told him I did not know that was going to happen. I was merely trying to make sure that Christopher felt comfortable talking to me. This accomplishment made me feel powerful, caring and patient. It added value to someone else's life and at the same time added value to my life. I do not know if Christopher was able to maintain his new speech. I left that barbershop and never saw him again. I pray that he learned something that he would be able to take through his life because I certainly did. That day I learned that everyone has something to say and it is a privilege to be able to articulate your thoughts clearly. I also learned that you are in a position to change someone's life and that anyone's life can change in a moment's notice. I believe that day was one of my biggest accomplishments because in my heart I felt great. I felt like a healer and that was priceless to me.

ACCOMPLISHMENT	YEAR	FEELING
1.		
2.		
3.		
4.		
5.		
6.		
7.		
8.		
9.		
10.		

Call to action:

1. Make a list of your accomplishments; note the year and the way it made you feel.
2. Choice which one you consider to be your biggest accomplishment and tell someone.
3. Repeat this affirmation daily
   "You have done great things and you will do more great things in due time."
4. Continue to remembering your accomplishments, big or small, and celebrate them.

Day 7 – Create the Day, Week, Month, Life

Did you know that you could create the perfect day and then do it over and over and over again? This chapter is about planning, plotting, charting and tracking but it is also about attracting what you want into your life. We often go through life complaining and worrying and clawing our way. That is no way to live. The truth is we create the life we want through our thinking and our choices. Not every choice will immediately turn into the result we dreamed of. Sometimes what we are working for will come after the storm like a rainbow.

When you have prepared and trained, when luck and blessings are sent your way, when you have positive thinking and have stopped trying to control everything, and when you have said please, the waters part and all of a sudden the gift is yours. The day is right and it turns into the perfect life. Not many people have figured out this equation. Some people have money but no love. Others have love but no money. Many people are smart but feel powerless. While others are powerful but fear people will not like them. When these people take their blinders off and see all that life has to offer, they will be able to live the perfect life.

Not everyone wants power or money but I would argue that all people want love in one way or another. We all have our gifts and our strengths. We know that there are just some things that come naturally to us. When it comes to those things that come harder to us, we either struggle through them or we don't do them at all. When it comes to creating the life you want, it may take you doing some of those things you are not good at. You may want something that is right now beyond your reach. When that happens you have to decide if you can live without it or determine what you are willing to sacrifice to get it. Right now I want you to make a list of sacrifices you have made. No matter how big or small they were, write them down. No matter how long ago they were, write them down.

I am not going to pretend like I know but others have said that we have to sacrifice something to get what we want. I guess we have to make a trade with the universe to show that we really value it. My goal in life is to have as little struggle and sacrifice as possible. Judging by what others have said that may mean that I get little reward as well. If sacrifice and struggle are directly related to our reward, that means I am setting myself up for mediocrity. I do not subscribe to this philosophy. I believe that you can create a great day, week, month and life with little struggle and little sacrifice. You have to commit to waiting for all the elements of the equation to come together, but you will eventually have what you want and be happy.

First I will help you recall because sometimes we forget the pain we have been through and sacrifice becomes a way of life. Sacrifice can be as simple as taking the family to Six Flags instead of taking that vacation to the Grand Canyon. While Six Flags is fun, it lacks the culture, education and majestic experience that the Grand Canyon would give your family; therefore it is a sacrifice. Most people think of sacrifice as lack, such as going hungry or without necessities. While that is the ultimate sacrifice, we are talking about all sacrifices, big or small. What is your sacrifice? What things have you given up to get what you want or to get through life? Have you let go of your hobbies? Have you changed your lifestyle? Have you done things that you were not proud of because you felt it was the only way? Recognize the sacrifices you have made. ***Write them below:***

_____

_____

_____

_____

_____

_____

_____

_____

_____

_____

_____

_____

_____

_____

_____

_____

Now that you have gotten those things out of your head and off of your chest, think about how much more you want to give up. There are probably some things that seemed like sacrifices at the time but in hindsight you see that they were necessary for the bigger picture. What is your life worth? What is your happiness worth?

Creating the perfect day is about knowing what that is. First find your perfect day, week, month and life. What is the perfect day to you? Is it when you can predict what will happen? Is it when every day is different? Is it full of work or is there some pleasure mixed in there? Are you alone or with company and what company would you like to keep? Do not let your current circumstance affect your answer. We are going to start with your work day. What does the ideal typical work day look like for you?

Write down what that day looks like. Break it down into sections: morning, afternoon, evening, night. I will start you off. What time would your day start? It's up to you. Do not feel pressured to write what you think others want you to say. You do not have to share this with anyone else if you do not want to. This is to help you determine what you really want, so make sure you write it down. What activity would you do first? Who would you work with? Are you the leader or an assistant? What makes you happy when you are working? What would make you feel like it was the perfect work day.

Morning: (*What is your morning like? When do you awaken, what do you eat, what do you do before 12pm?*)

_____

_____

_____

_____

_____

_____

_____

_____

_____

Afternoon: (*What is your afternoon like, what do you eat, who eats with you, are you working or playing?*)

_____

_____

_____

_____

_____

_____

_____

_____

Evening: (*What have you accomplished so far? Is the day exciting or laid back?*)

_____

_____

_____

_____

_____

_____

_____

_____

Night: (*How does your day end? Do you stay up late or go to sleep early? Who is with you?*)

_____

_____

_____

_____

_____

_____

_____

_____

Now that you have clearly written out your ideal workday, write down your ideal day off. Are there activities or are you completely relaxed? Are you doing hobbies or are you doing chores? Do you blend some things together or do you focus on one thing at a time? Are you with friends and family or are you alone? Take this time to write what you would like the perfect day off to be. Remember it is not about what someone else wants you to do. It is about what you want to do and what you feel will make you happy. What will make you the person you want to be with the life you want to live? Again break it down into sections and even if every section is the same write it down now.

Morning:

_____
_____
_____
_____
_____
_____
_____
_____

Afternoon:

_____
_____
_____
_____
_____
_____
_____
_____

Evening:

_____
_____
_____
_____

_____

_____

_____

_____

<u>Night</u>:

_____

_____

_____

_____

_____

_____

_____

Now that you have talked about your perfect work day and off day, write down how the fundamentals of this day will make you feel. As you write these feelings down, I want you to visualize it. Smell the ocean air on your boat. See the water; what color is it? Are your children there? If so, hear their voices. If not, hear the sounds that make you feel comfortable. How does that work week make you feel? Do you feel powerful, supported, respected, loved, strong or tired? How do you want to feel at the end of the day? Excited, anxious about tomorrow, quiet, victorious, or mild. Is your work hard? Does a hard work day sound perfect to you? Is your work thought provoking? Do your hands hurt, is your brain full, or is your body tense? Is your head clear at the end of the day or full of thought? What are you feeling and why do you want that feeling? Visualize it. Feel….

After you finish writing, sit and feel what you have written down. Do not think! Feel and visualize yourself doing the things you said you want to do. Let yourself feel each activity. If it makes you smile, go ahead and smile. When the emotions well-up inside you, let them. The feeling of doing exactly what you want to do is incredible. Let yourself feel it.

One step at a time you can start living the life you desire. You can create the perfect day with your thoughts and actions. When all the elements come together, you should be ready to get what you asked for. Each element plays a part in the bigger picture and in creating the life you desire. To help you remember, I will break down the elements for you. When you have prepared and trained, this element is about being in the condition to have the life that you want. If you need a degree to pursue your career of choice, then get it. If you need to have a certain type or amount of experience, go after it. If you need to know things that nobody else knows, learn them.

When you have positive thinking, life responds to what you send out. If you send out negative energy about how bad you feel and what is bad in your life, you will get more of it. What you focus on expands. Focus on the good in your life. Focus on the good in the world around you. Focus so that you can bring more of it into your life. Additionally, stop trying to control everything. This is complicated because you do need to maintain a certain amount of management over your life. However, you do not have to control everything. Instead, you should control your reactions, feelings and thoughts. React positively and calculated. Think positive and feel good about what you have and what you have coming.

Luck and blessings are sometimes sent our way. Things that you wanted occur when you least expect it. You do not have to work or worry about it; it just happens without your permission or assistance. Sometime things just work in your favor. The universe has many blessings to give out so you have to be ready and willing when it is your turn. Do not turn down or pass up your blessing. Be grateful and use it wisely. Sometimes it takes a long time for all the elements to come together and sometimes it happens quickly. The secret is being ready when it happens. The secret is being thankful all the time so that you can get your gift faster. If you say thank you and please during the entire process, you will get what you are asking for. Just make sure you are acting in accordance with your request.

This advice about creating your perfect day is the absolute hardest. This is when you have to only do the things that work toward creating your perfect day. If you did not list gossiping about your co-workers as part of your perfect day, then do not do it anymore. It is counter- productive anyway. You do not send out positive energy when you are speaking negatively about others. Also, it is energy you could use to work toward your life's purpose.

Your decision making has to come from a place that is centered in your perfect day. When you make decisions from this moment forward, you should first think about the day, week, month and life you are creating and decide if this will help you get there. If you are considering a job, first consult your list. Will this job help you get to your perfect day? It may not happen tomorrow but if you can see how the job plays a role in the bigger picture than take it. If the job does not fit into your plan, do not take it. You will find yourself back at square one starting over because you are still trying to create the day, week, month and life of your dreams.

Creating the day, week, month, life you desire is not about utopia. It does not mean that you will never have a bad moment or that you will never have another problem. You may encounter a problem, but the life you lead will also have the solution to that problem. The perfect life is being able to handle whatever comes your way. It is being prepared and grateful. It is about understanding your blessings and sharing them with others. It is about making a commitment to yourself and your family and sticking with it.

You say you want to be happy and now you are making moves to learn more about what happiness is to you. With this in mind you can create what you want in your life so you can repeat it. Sometimes you will forget it and you will find that trouble will sneak in. When that happens, remind yourself of how this principle works. Read over your creation and bring it back to life.

Today is the first day of your perfect life. Change the way you think about your life, change the way you feel about your life and change the things you do in your life. You know how you want to feel, now go out there and get it.

Call to action:
1. Create your perfect work day
2. Create your perfect off day
3. Write down how the perfect day will feel
4. Make decisions that will lead to your perfect day.

Day 8 – Bucket list

This chapter is to give you a chance to look at your desires in black and white. This will allow you to know for sure what you want to do. We call this list the "bucket list." It is a list of all the things you would like to do before you kick the bucket. You are going to go one day so before you do have some fun, do something exciting and love the life you have.

This is not a list of things you think you should write down because other people have done it. It is a list of what *you* really want and what *you* truly desire to do. It is a list of things that will make you feel satisfied and happy at the end. If you knew when your last day would be, how would you live your life? What things would you make sure you accomplished? I am going to ask you to pick a date; any date. It does not matter. It can be 2 years from now or 42 years from now, any month and any day you choose.

Write down this random date that pops into your head. Do not think too hard about it. Just make it up. Have fun with it.

Month: _____ Day: _____ Year: _____

Now let us pretend that this is your last day living. I know it is scary to think about it; so don't. This chapter is about living not dying; so think about how great it is going to be to live out your list. Now that you have a date, what things would you like to do and accomplish before this date? You can write down as many as you like. I am giving you space on the next two pages but if you need more, feel free to write your heart out.

Use this space and the space on the next page to be creative:

{Space for you to create}

_____
_____
_____
_____
_____
_____
_____
_____
_____
_____
_____
_____
_____
_____
_____
_____
_____
_____
_____
_____
_____
_____
_____
_____
_____
_____
_____
_____
_____
_____
_____
_____

The idea here is to get them out of your head and on paper so that you can start doing them. You do not have to do them in any certain order. You should try to get them all done but because we really do not know when that random date will be, we should live our lives working to check off as many as we can. If you do not get to accomplish them all, that is ok. Maybe your friends or family members will find this list and help you accomplish other items on it by doing them in your name.

As you accomplish things, literally take a pen and scratch them off. Write the date next to them. I encourage you to tell someone about it as well. Tell the story of your adventure. It may be as small as visiting the small town where your parents met or as big as climbing a mountain. Either way, it is your adventure and you can make it as exciting and story book as you want. You're creating it.

The bucket list is made up of activities that should be your goal to conquer. The list may never be complete because if you are like me, you will continue to think of new things you want to do and accomplish. That is ok. In fact, it is even better because it means you are continuing to dream bigger and bigger. It means you are living and have found what makes you happy and you want more of it. There is nothing wrong with that. I am so excited for you. I know what it feels like to scratch things off. When you start doing it, you cannot wait to get to the next thing. Have fun and live out your bucket list. Feel free to email me your list and your stories as you fulfill it. Email me at consultation@kinecorder.com, subject: **bucket list**.

Day 9 – Things I like

This chapter should be nothing but fun. In this chapter you are writing down all the things you like. It is your personal list and you do not have to share it with anyone if you do not want to. However, if you have a significant other, you may want to show them so that they will be more aware of your likes. Many times in relationships we know just how to tell someone what we do not like but we have a hard time expressing what we like. We expect them to read our minds when we have not even read our own minds. This chapter will give you a chance to read your mind and to search your soul, mind and heart for the things that make you happy. You will make a list of everything you can think of from material to spiritual things.

You may end up with a "Things I Like" list that is a mile long or barely a whole sheet of paper. Either is okay. Even if you only like it once in a while, you can write it down. For instance, I do not enjoy ice cream that much. However, I do get a craving for it every once in a while and when I do, I want my favorite flavor only. Have you ever made a list of the things you like? Do you know what you like? I want you to break the list up into physical, mental, emotional and spiritual likes. For example, your spiritual likes may be meditating or going to church. Your mental likes may be reading or learning. Your emotional likes may be watching your children sleep or getting a hug from someone who loves you. A physical like is eating a certain food or doing a certain activity. I am sure you have many of those. As you know, if you run out of room here feel free to grab some paper and continue your list.

You can be as general or as specific as you want to be as you are writing. Let us start with the one that I think will be the easiest for you. Write down some of your many physical likes. List anything that feels physical to you like eating, playing, working, etc. These are things that make you feel good physically or things that make you feel physically powerful. Working out, making love, playing a sport or even eating your favorite food.

My physical likes:

Example: Tennis

1.
2.
3.
4.
5.
6.
7.
8.
9.

Now write down the things that you like to do that are more mental than physical. Write things that make you feel good mentally or make you feel smart, powerful or informed. Maybe there is a magazine that you read for mental stimulation. Maybe you are learning something new. Conversations can be mentally stimulating too. What mental likes do you have? List them here. Don't feel any pressure to fill in all the spaces; you have your whole life to do that. You may discover something that you like mentally that you did not even know you liked. When you do, add it to your list.

My mental likes:

Example: Reading the newspaper

    1.
    2.
    3.
    4.
    5.
    6.
    7.
    8.
    9.

You probably have it by now. Write down your emotional likes. These are things like affection, love or compliments. What do you like that makes you feel good emotionally? I think listening to music can be emotional. For me watching movies is emotional because it is the time when I stop thinking and just feel.

My emotional likes:

Example: Hugging

    1.
    2.
    3.
    4.
    5.
    6.
    7.
    8.
    9.

I know you have it but I will still give you a little assistance in listing your spiritual likes. These likes are things like attending church or meditating. This may even be giving charitable contributions or anything else that warms your spirit. Your emotional likes and spiritual likes may overlap. That is okay. Do not feel bad if you write something down twice. That just means you really like it and it fulfills you in more than one way. Keep writing and discovering what you like, especially in this area. We often know our favorite food or movie or past time, but we rarely think about feeding ourselves spiritually and what we like on a deeper level. Take the time to do it now.

My Spiritual like:

Example: Meditating

1.
2.
3.
4.
5.
6.
7.
8.
9.

As I mentioned before, this list will continue to grow because you will discover new things that you like to do. You will also start to remember things that you like to do that you did not think of or that you haven't done in a while. Write them down so that you can remember to do them. You want to use these things to bring more happiness into your life. If you are doing things that make you happy, you will be happy. If you utilize your list, you will make all four aspects of life more complete. The list will assist you in knowing what you need in order to feel completely happy. Once you know what makes you happy you can do more of it.

Now that you are clear on many of the things that bring you happiness, you should start doing more of them today. While you are starting over, implement some of your likes and it will enable you to enjoy the process more. It will help you get to a place of peace faster than you had in the past. When you know what you like, you are able to get more of it and you are able to express it to others.

Call to action:

1. Make your list of physical, mental, emotional and spiritual likes.
2. Start doing these things more often. Start on your reward days that will come later in the book.
3. Start expressing what you really like to the people in your life.

Day 10 – Reward Yourself

Today you are going to give yourself a day off to do one of the things that you discovered you liked. You can choose from your "bucket list" or you can choose from your "things I like list." This day is about you. This day is to celebrate all the things you have discovered in the last 9 chapters.

Before you take the day to reward yourself, you need to write and recite an affirmation. This affirmation should encompass some of the things you learned about yourself in the past and while reading this book. Affirmations are positive. You should write down a few and begin reciting them today and every day. You can write new ones whenever you like or keep the same ones as long as you like. I will share with you one of my affirmations and I will give you some examples of how to start your affirmations.

My affirmations:

I feel peaceful as I enjoy speaking, writing and consulting my clients. I love assisting people in learning how to enjoy their lives more. I smile every time I check my voicemail, email and bank account. I receive messages that encourage me to continue to do my life's work. I have more than enough to take care of myself and the people around me.

I am the happiest woman in the world. My life is full of abundance and blessings. I am in a relationship where we love, like, respect and live with each other harmoniously. We take care of our business and we take care of each other mentally, physically, emotionally and spiritually.

One of the affirmations was about business life and one is about personal life. Speak peace and happiness into all aspects of your life. I want you to take the time out to write down your affirmation today. You may not get it exactly right. You may begin it now and think of something else later. It took time for me to discover the things I wanted to include in my affirmation.

Use my affirmation as an example and let it give you some ideas, but write your own. Here are some words that can help you get started on your affirmation.

I am

I enjoy

I love

I have faith

I feel proud

I am excited about

I feel peaceful as I

I smile when I

I have accomplished

I am happy that

I am grateful

You can write as many as you like. You should make sure they are all positive and speak good things into your life. They are almost like prayers but instead of asking, you are affirming. You are speaking as if you have it now. You are thankful and feeling the experience as if it is your life now. This will help you to continue to create the life you desire. Remember to recite them daily. Start now and edit them until you feel like they express your true desires and feelings. You will see it start to unfold in your life and that is when you will understand that you deserve to have your perfect lifestyle.

My Affirmations:

_____

_____

_____

_____

_____

_____

_____

_____

_____

_____

_____

_____

_____

_____

_____

You wrote down affirmations that have significant meaning to you. These affirmations express how you want to feel and what you want to accomplish. Edit them as your wants and accomplishments change but continue to recite them daily. You can leave them in this book and open it to read them or you can write or type them out and place them in a place where you will see them. Some people put there affirmations on the bathroom mirror where they will see them every morning. I put mine at the front door so I will see them on my way out. Put yours wherever you think they will have the most effect on you; in your car, your appointment book or on your computer desk top. You can put them in one place or in several different places. The point is to do whatever gives you the greatest feeling.

When you read the title of this chapter, you may think this is a free day. It is. Although you are still doing some work toward your ultimate goal, you get to do something fun and rewarding at the same time.

When you have done something good you should reward yourself because this is how you keep going. At this point you have gotten through the first part of this book. This is the training part. We have trained your mind to think positive and we have you on your way to the track meet.

The next section will be "take your mark". You will start to focus, plan and see where you are going. The things you did in training will help you take your mark. They will help you focus and plan. You are doing great. Keep up the good work. Enjoy this day and put your running shoes on when you get back from rewarding yourself because you are ready.

Call to action:

1. Write your affirmations.
2. Begin reciting your affirmations daily.
3. Do something today that makes you happy. Use your "bucket list" or "things I like" list.

Day 11 – Why you want it

When I was a Barber Stylist I would sometimes make house calls. One day I was at a client's house and he was reading the Robb Report, a magazine for the luxury lifestyle, while I was cutting his hair. This client told me to get a subscription. He said it is not enough to know that you want to have money. You have to know what you want to buy. That is what will motivate you; not the money itself but what it can bring you. This client was the kind of man that you would not know had that kind of wisdom or would be kind enough to share it with someone like me. Taking the advice of that client, I got a subscription to the Robb Report. I made a decision on how much money I wanted to make that year and I also made a list of things I wanted to do with that money. Taking his advice a step further, I then decided to write down why I wanted it. I figured the "why" is what keeps you going when the "what" is not enough. The "what" is a brand new car; the "why" is for perfect transportation back and forth to work.

Only you know why you want it. There are often things that happened to you "way back when" that set the why in place. Some have stories about teachers telling them they were never going to be anything. Others have parents or grandparents that they want to take care of. While others just want to say "na, na, na, nanah." Whether you like showing off or your heart is to take care of a village in Africa, your why is personal. There is a reason why you have it. Think back to some of the things you thought about doing as a child. Take the realistic ones and make them your why. We know that you cannot have all the money in the world like you use to wish for or cure all the sick, but you can do your part.

In this chapter, you are going to write down "what you want" and "why you want it." They will probably never change. However, the "what you want" may change as time goes on and as you accomplish some of your goals. You may also find that the "what" wasn't all it was cracked up to be and you will adjust that. The "why" on the other hand, is usually deeper than just a simple need. It is something you feel very strongly about. Most people know their why if they give it some thought. You are going to make a few lists in this chapter. You will make a list of your needs, wants and feelings that you have right now or that are on-going. Some of your needs will be material and some will be psychological or physiological. Love and acceptance are physiological needs. Houses, cars and clothes are material needs.

I am not going to ask you to say whether it is material or physiological or psychological. That part is not important. Making sure you fulfill the need is. You are making a list of what you need right now. What would you like to have more of in your life? (ie: love, food, money, security, control, help, patience), How would you feel if these needs were added to your life? The feelings will tell you what the need is. The need is the void you feel. The need is the thing you are trying to attract in your life. Do you feel lonely, happy, peaceful, separated or grateful? Do you have a need to be wanted, needed, supported, appreciated or vulnerable? Are you feeling scared, nervous, excited, or inquisitive? Perhaps you feel like superman or superwoman or maybe you feel like the weight on your shoulders is too much. Once you finish the list, write a paragraph to describe the way you feel right now. Then write a sentence about the way you would like to feel. Remember as you are writing the needs and feelings that they do not all have to be negative. So focus on the positive too. You may be happy or peaceful or excited or pretty or any number of positive feelings. The needs you have are still there. It is ok if you are feeling conflicted. You may have a need that seems to contradict one of your feelings. That is okay too. You are going to have different feelings. You are going to want different things at different times and that is fine. Take this time to write down your feelings, needs and what you believe will help you fulfill the need.

NEED	FEELING	WHAT WILL FULFILL THIS NEED
More space	*Comfort*	*A bigger house*
Affection	*Attractive*	*If my wife would touch me more*

Write a paragraph about your feelings, needs and fulfillment. When you finish the paragraph that describes your needs and feelings, write a sentence about how you want to feel. It may be the opposite of what you are feeling now or it may be similar. It is your life and you are free to feel however you feel. There is no right or wrong. This exercise is to discover not to judge. Describe what you are feeling right now.

_____
_____
_____
_____
_____
_____
_____
_____

Now describe how you would like to feel.

_____
_____
_____
_____

WHAT YOU WANT	WHY YOU WANT IT
My own business	*So my family members will have jobs*
More income	*So my children can go to any college they like*

Having your needs fulfilled is a big part of being happy and a big part of getting them fulfilled, is identifying the needs. If you know what you want and need, you are more likely to get it. You will be able to express it better and to identify it when you have it. If you cannot pin point the need, you will never know how to fix it. It is just like when you are sick and go to the doctor. He is unable to diagnose the problem if he does not know what is wrong. He must first ask you a series of questions that will lead to his diagnosis.

When you answer the questions and he still does not know why, he will attempt to solve the problem although he may not come to a conclusion. You go on trying and taking more medicine but until the doctor knows what it is, you may not get better. As he continues to monitor and examine you, he may come up with the right solution. The faster he figures out what the problem is, the faster he can begin administering the treatment which leads to the cure.

This chapter is very important because it will set the precedence for the next few chapters to come. This chapter will help you understand yourself better and it will help you get to the bottom of the longing you have inside. Be willing to express yourself. Talk it through with someone or on your own. Pay attention to what you are complaining about. You do not want to complain; you want to live so it's important to find out what you need to live. When you begin living, you feel like a different person.

You may get what you need from someone or something that is already in your life or you may need to go searching for more. First, you have to get down to the need. What do you need to have more of in your life? When you go on date after date, what are you really searching for? When you work late hours, what are you trying to get? When you try everything not to go home, what do you think is out there that you do not have at home? If you have not figured it out, keep going because you need to know what feelings you are experiencing in order to fulfill the need you have.

From here on out there should be no complaining. There should only be expressions. You can state the problem but you need to have the solution to follow. You know what you need now and you have a good idea of what will help you feel how you want to feel. If you are open with yourself and the people around you, things will start to change and you will get what you need.

Do not be afraid. You may discover that the current company you keep is unable to fulfill your needs or your current job is not able to give you the fulfillment you desire. You are looking for change; this is the realization that you have to do it. If you want a different life then you will have to do something different. Even if you are fearful, just do it anyway. That is what it means to be brave. When you are afraid and you do not let the fear stop you, you are brave. I should also tell you that it is okay to feel. Allow yourself to experience every emotion. Do not get out of control with your emotions; just feel them, identify them and get on with your life of fulfilling your needs. Keep in mind how your actions and feelings affect others. Be kind, be aware and be your best. Feel, explore, live.

Call to action:
1. Write down your need, what feeling you want and what will help you get that need fulfilled.
2. Write down what you want (material or otherwise) and why you want it.
3. Start sharing your needs with the people around you.

Day 12 – Your Purpose in Life

What is your purpose in life? This is a deep and very important question that most of us spend our whole lives trying to figure out. Some people never actually get it, while others get it, complete it, and feel great doing it. It is time to be one of those people. Do you already know your life purpose? If so, you're probably tempted to go straight to the exercise. You could, but do not do that (Do not pass go and do not collect $200.) This is not a get out of jail free card. This is a walk, not a sprint, through a very important part of your life.

Knowing what your life's purpose is will make this chapter easier. If you do not, then you may be irritated by the opening question because it may seem impossible to answer. But you should be able to do it by the end of the chapter or at least by the end of this book. Maybe this is the first time you have really taken the time to think about yourself in this way. Maybe you have been taking care of others and at that time, *that* was your life purpose; but now it is time to choose another one.

Well we know you are not Mother Theresa, Dr. Martin Luther King Jr., nor Barrack Obama. Since we know who you are not, let us find out who you are, what you are going to do in the world and with your life. Your life purpose could be to raise the next Barrack Obama or to start the next technological advancement. Either way, you are an important part of the world however big or small your contribution may be. Some of us believe that we have to go down in history to matter. That is not true. We can recycle responsibly, teach children to write, make people beautiful or clean the offices of the biggest companies in the world. Whatever your purpose is, it belongs to you and it is important. Be sure to find some prestige in your life. Feel good about what you do. Act as if you are the greatest. Do your best and make the thing you enjoy your life purpose.

Now we are going to answer a few questions that will help you determine the type of work and life purpose you would enjoy most. Keep in mind that your life purpose does not have to be your life work. They can be two different things. You can use these exercises and this book to find out both. Your life purpose can be a hobby to you or a charitable contribution. It could be what you spend 20% of your life doing. That 20% could make your life 100% enjoyable.

What have you done that has made you feel the most happy and meaningful? Have you ever done anything that made you feel absolutely peaceful? Have you done something that made you smile as you went to sleep at night? Have you experienced something where, like my mentor says, the sun could not come up fast enough for you to get back to it?

If you are not able to think of anything right away feel free to go back to Chapter 9 and see if you can get some ideas. Enjoy this exercise as much as you can. Do not let it bring you down if you are not able to think of anything right away. If some of these exercises are difficult for you, it just means that you are right on-time. This really is the right time to start over and get the life you want.

Write down the times when you felt like you were doing something that made you happy.

_____

_____

_____

_____

_____

_____

_____

_____

Do you see anything that these activities had in common? Were there people in common? Was there a type of place that was common? What feeling did you get from each activity and which ones gave you the greatest joy?

_____
_____
_____
_____
_____
_____
_____
_____

What are you naturally good at? What do you do well without even trying? Maybe there is one thing or maybe there are several. Some people are multi-talented; others are extremely good at a specific thing. Either way, write down your natural talents. What comes easy to you?

_____
_____
_____
_____
_____
_____
_____
_____

What are you skilled at? Name the things that you have learned over the years that you have perfected. Maybe it was something your grandfather taught you or something you learned in a trade school. What skills do you possess?

_____
_____
_____
_____
_____
_____
_____
_____

Write down the things you love to do; not the things you like. You wrote that down already. This is a shorter list. What do you love to do on your day off or what would you take off of work to do? What are the things that make you want to live longer? It is your list so be honest. Write it down even if it is something that most people do not know about you.

_____
_____
_____
_____
_____
_____
_____
_____

When do you feel at your best? When do you have the most energy? What makes you want to keep going?

_____
_____
_____
_____
_____
_____
_____

Do you remember a time when you felt really good about yourself? What were you doing? Who were you with? What did you look like? What made you feel so good? When do you feel the best about yourself?

_____
_____
_____
_____
_____
_____
_____

What do people usually ask for your help with? What do the people around you compliment you on? What do they say you are really good at? What thing, skill or characteristic do you have that most people don't?

_____

_____

_____

_____

_____

_____

_____

_____

Go back and read your answers. Do you see any overlap? Do you notice any patterns? What are the commonalities of the things you wrote about? Do you see yourself as a great leader or have you been great at assisting? Assistants do not get as much applause as leaders but their job is equally important. Without the assistant, the leader is sometimes helpless. Do you achieve best in a group or on your own? Are you good at thinking fast and reacting or is your gift slowly calculating all the possibilities and strategically coming to a conclusion? Are you artistic or scientific? Do you like the outdoors or do you prefer interiors? Is geography your thing or do you know history like a college professor? Do you think about how beautiful and energizing the sunrise is or do you love watching the moon and stars in the still of the night? What is it that drives you? What were you put on this earth to do?

Pretend that life starts over today. You have all the knowledge you have acquired over your life but you get to start over. But here is the catch: You are on a private island that belongs to you. For the first month you will be the only one there. What will you miss the most?

_____

_____

_____

_____

The next month your help will arrive. Now you have a chef, butler, chauffeur and a personal assistant. What is your first order of business for your assistant?

_____
_____
_____
_____

What will you tell the chief to prepare?

_____
_____
_____
_____

What should your butler clean first?

_____
_____
_____
_____

What kind of car do you have? Where should the chauffeur take you?

_____
_____
_____
_____

What gender are your chef, butler, chauffeur and personal assistant? Why?

_____
_____
_____
_____

Now a plane is going to bring 12 people to your private island. You get to choose what each one of them will do. You can choose to be the leader of this island or you can sit back and chill. You can be a parent or you can chose not to assign any of the people as your children. It is your life so you make it happen. What will your job be and what will you do for fun? You now live with four female adults, four male adults, two 17 year olds, one 10 year old and one 4 year old.

What is your purpose on this island?

_____
_____
_____
_____
_____
_____
_____
_____
_____
_____
_____
_____
_____

Is your purpose on this island the same as your purpose in the real world? If not, how is it different? Why is it different?

_____
_____
_____
_____
_____
_____
_____
_____

Now that you are back to reality, write down your new purpose in life. Write as much as you like and be specific.

_____
_____
_____
_____

_____

_____

_____

_____

_____

_____

_____

_____

_____

_____

_____

_____

_____

Call to action:

1. Answer all the life purpose questions.
2. If someone tells you they want to know their life purpose, tell them about this book.
3. Start doing things that will lead to you living out your life purpose.

Day 13 – Set Goals

You set goals and write them down to remind yourself of what you want to accomplish and when. Setting goals is a big part of successfully starting over and getting what you want. In chapter 7 you created your ideal day, week, month and life. In chapter 12 you discovered your purpose in life. In order to reach those two ideas, you will have to set goals. I am sure you have set goals in the past, many of which you have completed successfully. This time will not be much different from that. The only difference this time is that you are going to use all the principles you have already read about and a few more to reach your goals faster and more accurately.

When we do not accomplish our goals it sets a series of events into motion. We tell ourselves that we really did not want it anyway, we begin a habit of not finishing what we start and we start to second guess ourselves. When this happens, we build up a guard of distrust. The next time we set a goal we do not see it as important so we do not finish it. That is why seeing your goals through is important. You do not want to get into the habit of quitting or distrusting yourself.

Goals should be specific, actionable, realistic and measurable. Specific, so that you will know exactly what you want and design a plan that will get you there. The goal should be actionable so that you will know what tasks will get you to your goal. Also, you should always be realistic otherwise you are setting yourself up for failure. However, it is only impossible until somebody does it so do not let me limit you. Being realistic does not mean stop dreaming. Dream big! Just have a strategy that can help you bring those dreams to reality. Your goals should also be measurable because you need to know when you are close. This will keep you going. If you say you want to lose 50lbs, it is easy to see when you are close. But if your goal is to lose weight it will be harder to measure when you have reached your goal. Goals should also be broken down into categories. There are short term, mid-term goals and long term goals. Short term goals happen in 30, 60, 90 days. If you were in college your short term goal might be completing your assignments, getting to know your teacher or getting an A out of the class. Your mid-term goal might be to maintain a certain grade point average or to do an exchange student program. Your long term goal might be to graduate with honors. All of these goals are specific, actionable, realistic and measurable.

It is your turn now. First take a look back at some of the things we have already discussed. Look at chapter 12 and determine what your goals should be. Remember you will have short term, mid-term and long term goals. They will not all be big; some will be small. You need those too. Look at the things you like and the self-evaluation. Set goals that are realistic but remember to aim high. You are powerful and you can make things happen. Below you will write down your goals. Do not worry about how you will reach them or who will help you or how much it will cost right now. Just write down the goals you want to accomplish. Stay optimistic when making the list. You know what you want out of life so now it is time to make the plan. You have accomplished goals before. These are new ones and you will accomplish them too. Starting over is not a bad thing. It is a chance to get you back on track or moving in the right direction.

Write a list of goals. Next you will prioritize. Put your head down and as they come out write them down. Do not stop yourself; you can scratch some off later if you want to but for now just write them all down.

<u>My goals</u>:

# in priority	Goal

Now from the list above, prioritize your goals. Put your goals in order breaking them down into short term, mid-term and long term. Remember your short term goals can be completed in 1-90 days. Your mid-term goals will fall between 3-12 months. And your long term goals will be 1-5 years or more. When you are starting over you want to see the big picture and you want to handle the decisions based on the way you want the big picture to look. What you do today will have an effect on tomorrow.

SHORT TERM GOALS

(Goals I would like to attain in the next 1-90 days)

1.
2.
3.
4.
5.
6.
7.
8.
9.

This list may not be very long because short term goals take focus and you cannot fragment yourself too much or you will not get them done. Going back to our previous example, if you are planning to get an A out of your class you may have to cut some other things out. You cannot spend as much time with your friends because you need to spend time with your books.

Take a look at your list above. Prioritize your list and come up with your next set of goals. What things will you accomplish in the next 3-12 months? Remember you are just listing them now; not setting your strategy.

MID-TERM GOALS

(Goals I would like to attain in the next 3-12 months)

1.
2.
3.
4.
5.
6.
7.
8.
9.

The list you just made should be the things that will help you understand the path to your long term goals. These goals will put you in a position to feel better about your life. This will give you the strength you need to get to your long term goals. Before you plan your strategy, finish writing out all of your goals. Move on to your long term goals now and continue to do the same thing you did for short and mid-term. It will all come together soon. When you are able to see your goals clearly you are able to reach them faster.

LONG TERM GOALS

(Goals I would like to attain in the next 1-5 years)

1.
2.
3.
4.
5.

6.

7.

8.

9.

Now take a look at all your goals. Do you see how they all work together? Do you see how you can clearly get them done? Once you get one set of goals out of the way, you can move on to the next. One thing I need you to keep in mind, and forgive me if this sounds elementary, is when you finish your short term goals you will make your mid-term goals your new short term goals. Some of your long term goals will then move up to mid-term goals and so on. You probably already knew that but I mentioned it because part of the reason we do not accomplish our goals is because we get half way there and stop. We keep saying when this or that happens I will pursue my goal. I will save more money when I have a higher paying job but we are not looking for a new job. You have to take action.

In the next few chapters we will begin to strategize, plan and break down your goals. We will put together your daily activity list in order to meet your goals. Before you do that, take some time to look at all your goals. Add in a few more if you forgot any. Scratch off some that you changed your mind about. You can put them back later if you decide you really do want to accomplish them. Visualize yourself accomplishing these goals and what it will feel like. Take one of your long term goals and see yourself there. Where are you? Who is there with you? What feeling do you have in your heart, in the pit of your stomach and in your soul?

Call to action:
1. Make a complete list of goals.
2. Break goals down into short term, mid-term and long term goals.
3. Visualize one of your long term goals.

Day – 14 Tasks

For many people, goals are too big and they have a hard time seeing the trees for the forest. When you are always looking at the big picture you have a hard time breaking it down into all the tiny little parts that have to happen first. Like in our first example, if your goal was to graduate from college with honors, how do you achieve that? If your goal was to build a forest where would you begin? You have to start by planting the first tree. Break it down into smaller parts so it is not so scary. There are things that have to happen first in order to start a forest just as there are things that have to happen in order to graduate with honors.

Both goals are attainable but they must first be broken down into tasks. We already talked about this when you were categorizing your goals. Think about what tasks you would have if you wanted to graduate with honors. You would have to pass your classes with A's which means you would have to do well on all assignments. You would need to study and get a tutor or study partner if you need help. Whatever your goals are, breaking them down into tasks and having a strategy is what is going to get that goal completed.

The first thing I want you to do is to tell the story about how you are going to accomplish your goal. Take one of your short term goals and just think it through. Write below as if you are talking to someone and let them know how you will get the short term goal accomplished. Be specific. Tell how you will work on it daily and the steps you would take. Talk about your deadlines and any help you will need to get it done. Ask yourself the same questions that you think someone else would ask you. Take one of your goals now and write out the strategy.

This is the story about how I plan to reach my goal. *In order to reach my goal I.....* _____

_____
_____
_____
_____
_____
_____
_____

Writing your story out is a way for you to think through all the steps necessary to reach your goal. All of this may sound silly to you or make you feel childish but it is a way to help you visualize what you need to do to get it done. When you talk it through you can see holes in the plan that need to be filled. You can feel confident about your journey because you know that you have thought it through.

The next thing you are going to do is write down three goals and then list all the tasks you have to complete in order to meet your goal. Next to each task, write the date you would like to complete it and check it off once you have completed it. To reference our example from earlier, if you want to graduate from college then you have to enroll. Colleges have deadlines so set your deadlines prior to theirs. There will be some things that you do not have control over but try to schedule them into your strategy accordingly. Do not complain or waste your time trying to change them; work around them.

Goal 1 _____

TASKS

_____	_____
_____	_____
_____	_____
_____	_____
_____	_____
_____	_____

Goal 2 _____

TASKS

___ _____
___ _____
___ _____
___ _____
___ _____
___ _____

Goal 3 _____

TASKS

___ _____
___ _____
___ _____
___ _____
___ _____
___ _____

Call to action:

1. Write out a strategy story for one of your goals.
2. Write down three goals and the associated tasks to complete the goal with deadlines.
3. Check off your tasks as you complete them.

Day 15 – Strengths and Weaknesses

You may already know both your strengths and weaknesses or you may know your strengths but not your weaknesses or vice versa. Either way by the end of this chapter you will know both and you will understand why this knowledge is important.

Strength – where you are strong, what you are good at, what comes naturally to you or what you get compliments on. Your strengths can be things that you have been good at since you were a child or skills that you learned over the years. They can be characteristics, skills or personality traits. We should use our strengths as often as we can.

Make a list of your strengths. After you write down all the strengths you can think of, go back and write beside each one whether it is an emotional, mental, physical or spiritual strength. If you do not know, take a guess. If you think it falls under more than one category, write them both down.

STRENGTH	CATEGORY
Example: Thoughtful	Emotional
Example: Book Smart	Mental

If you did not have enough space, grab a piece of paper and keep going. This should not be a hard exercise; this should be enjoyable and power boosting. If you are having a difficult time writing, close your eyes and see what comes to you. Do not open your eyes until you are ready to write down your strengths.

Now for some of you, writing your weaknesses may be difficult. This may be because you are in denial or you are a perfectionist or you just do not like to think about it. It is okay; being weak at something does not make you a bad person. I am really bad at a few things like I have a short attention span. I am strong at planning, organizing and working quickly. But my attention span is weak and I have to keep moving.

Write down as many of your weaknesses as you can think of. You may find that some of your strengths are also weaknesses in certain situations. For example, I am a planner. When it comes to planning and organization, I am strong. But when it comes to being spontaneous I am weak. So my strength for organizing becomes a weakness if I need to be spontaneous.

List the areas where you are weak. Be sure to go back and list the category as well.

WEAKNESS	CATEGORY
Example: Thoughtful	*Emotional*
Example: Book Smart	*Mental*

I know that making this list can be hard. Admitting to yourself that you are selfish, a procrastinator, perfectionist, tyrant or lazy can be disheartening. I am not trying to discourage you; I am simply helping you identify your weaknesses so that you can use them in the next few chapters. When you know the problem, you can work toward the solution. Sometimes you will have to use your strengths to make your weaknesses better and this is why you have to identify your strengths too. This book is about looking at the entire picture; the real picture without any rose colored 3D glasses on. I do not want you to think you are more powerful than you are because then you will misjudge the work you need to do. I also do not want you to think you are less powerful than you are because then you will think you are not capable.

Be fair and honest with yourself. Strengths and weaknesses make us who we are but that does not mean we have to be judged by them. There is no right or wrong when it comes to strengths and weaknesses. We are not all created equally but because we all have strengths and weaknesses it all balances out.

Call to action:
1. Write down your strengths with the related category.
2. Write down your weaknesses with the related category

Day 16 – Needs

What do you need? Seriously, it is a legitimate question that we should always ask ourselves so that we can get what we want faster and feel happy. When you are pursuing a particular goal you may find that there are things you need help with. Take our example about graduating from college with honors. You may find you need a tutor in certain classes. You may be good in math but bad in English. If you fulfill the need, you get to your goal. If you do not fulfill the need, you may not get to your goal.

Everybody needs something. Some needs are emotional, some are physical, some are spiritual and some are mental. Many people are ashamed to have needs and have a hard time asking for help. You have to be okay with having needs. Often times we want to be superheroes and put all the weight of the world on our shoulders. When we do that we can end up failing. Teamwork can make things easier for everyone involved, especially if everyone gets to use their talents and strengths to reach the goal.

Write down as many needs as you can think of. They do not have to be immediate needs. They do not have to be big needs. You may or may not need all the space but you have it if you need it. Write as much as you can think of. Also, you may think of things later while you are reading this book or even after you finish. Some needs will be on-going and others will come and go. You may get some needs fulfilled and later have a need for it again. That is okay. As the world turns, so does your life and your needs. Write down all the needs you can think of.

NEED	

Call to action:

1. Write a list of all your needs. Include mental, physical, emotional or spiritual needs.
2. Scratch off needs as you fulfill them.
3. Add new needs if you discover them later.

Day 17 – Resources

You just finished making a list of all the challenges and needs you have right now. The next step is to figure out how to fill them, fix them or forget them. Take note of all your resources such as relationships, people you have worked with in the past, people who owe you favors, skills you can tap into, advantages, and even government assistance. Build your team of experts. There are people who know more than you do about a subject or whose strength is your weakness. Make sure you utilize the people around you to build a strong team that can help you professionally and personally. You are not an island. There are people around you who can make your life better. Utilize the good people and get rid of the bad. I know that is easier said than done, but at times it is necessary.

If you learn how to get people out of your life who aren't any good you will do yourself a big favor. Remember not to drag anyone else down either. If you are not a positive influence in your friends' lives then maybe you should remove yourself. Do not hold that friend back from their success and do not let anyone hold you back from yours. You do not have to carry anyone to the promise land. You can show them the way when you find it. When you discover that someone is bringing you down. Make sure you gently remove them from your life and except them back when you are sure they have learned how to be a good friend. When you know you have done your best in the relationship do not be afraid or feel guilty.

Take a look at your list of needs. Re-write that list now. This time, write down next to it whether you know someone that can help you with that need or challenge. Is there a government program, a work program, a co-worker, colleague, family member or neighbor who can be a resource to you? If so, make sure you prepare yourself mentally to receive the blessings that will come your way when you tell the universe what you need help with. Help is on the way.

NEED	RESOURCE

It is good to have people around you who are not only on your level but hopefully above you as well so that you can have someone to look up to. When I speak of levels, I am not speaking only of income level. I am always looking at all four aspects of life: mental, physical, emotional and spiritual.

Let's first talk about flushing out the complications. The people in your life who hold you down or take more than you are willing to give, are keeping you from succeeding. Are you ok with that? Are you willing to give up your life to the people around you? If not, then you need to find a way to put those friendships in the past. My aunt said something profound to me the day I graduated from high school. She said, "You know how you graduated from high school? Well, you graduate from people too. You didn't stay in high school after graduation, so don't try to stay in relationships with people you have already graduated from either." Once you have received your lesson or blessing, it may be time to move on. You be the judge. You know if you have had enough. Don't over stay your welcome in someone's life and don't let someone over stay their welcome in yours.

I put both of those out there because you may be the person who is taking more than you are giving. You may have discovered this in your self-evaluation or in the giver/taker chapter. If not, let's take a look at it now. Here is one sure fire way to tell - ask yourself, "do I have more people that owe me favors or more people I owe favors to?" If you owe a lot of people a lot of favors, then chances are you are the taker. That might not sound very good to you and if it doesn't, then make sure you are doing things to change it right now. Make sure that you make yourself a resource for someone. Be useful to the people around you and be honest about what is your fair share.

Look at it this way; either way, you might be in a good position. If you owe a lot of people favors, you are now in a position to not only repay them, but to show them how you have grown. The best part about this position is at least you know you have generous people around you who care about your success. Now, if you haven't cashed in your "friend card" lately, then you may be due for a favor or two. So ask away but be careful though. Spread out the requests. Don't beg and make sure you have something to give in return. *The two most important things I want you to remember: never take more than the person is comfortable giving and never take more than you are comfortable paying back.* If you follow those two rules, the situation should be fine.

Think about what is important and break down the team members. You always want someone around you who is wise and does the right thing while telling you what the best decision is based on who you are. This person is usually not afraid to tell you the truth. If you are unsure if you have that trait, make sure you add that person to your team; someone like grandma or a person who, as they say, has an old soul. This person can say "baby I see what you are trying to do but you're going about it the wrong way." They can pull your coat tail and they can give you some real life experiences. You need someone who can tell you when you are wrong even when you don't want to hear it. It's best if it's someone with finesse of course, but they need to be stern also so you will listen. It is good to have a "yes" person around you but having someone honest is more important. The "yes" person can come into your life later.

Find a good friend that can be your cheerleader and tell you when you have scored or done something right. Find someone who will visit you in the hospital for hours or someone who will tell the world about your accomplishments. Sounds kind of like a mother huh? Well it might be or it could just be a friend who has a mother-like heart. Find a Momma and keep her close.

You should also have a "Daddy Warbucks;" a rich friend, parent or relative who believes in you and who trusts you. This person is like grandpa. Grandpa will go into his pocket and pull out a dollar for you without hesitation. This is a good friend indeed. Now, if you have a friend like this be very careful not to get greedy. Their money is not your money. They do not owe you anything. If they give you something, it is out of the kindness of their own heart. If they do not give you any money, then maybe you have not proven yourself to be trustworthy or responsible. Grandpa can be a man or a woman. This person just has a supportive, giving heart with a bank account to support it.

Now, Grandma is going to tell you the truth about yourself but "Brotherman" is going to tell you the truth about the world. This person should have good common sense but more importantly, street smarts. They know how to smell a rat or a snake and they know what to do with them when they find one. It is good to have people in high and low places. You never know what you are going to need. Brotherman can tell you the way the world is because he (or she) has been there. Brotherman comes in handy, but can also be guilty of some of the things that he accuses other people of so be careful if you have one in your life. Be sure to know what you are working with. If you do not already know one, borrow one from someone else. This person does not embarrass easily. Brotherman is confident and cunning. Learn from Brotherman and keep one close.

Last on the list is the person who will pick up your dry cleaning, buy you lunch and bring it to your job when you cannot find the time to do it. This team member will cook you dinner or make you a pot of soup when you are sick. Lil' Sister is just plain old helpful. Now mama and grandma will make you soup too, but little sister knows the secrets nobody else knows. She can be Wonder Woman at times but she will also let you rescue her; but only if she really, really needs it. For men Lil' Sister may be a wife or ex-girlfriend. For women, Lil Sister may be your real sister or a best friend. Whoever she is, she is a great addition to the team. Do not live life without her. Everyone needs a Lil Sister in their life. She will not complain but be careful again. Do not wear Lil Sister out. She will break at some point and you do not want that point to be when you need her most. Lil Sister will be there for you so make sure you are there for her. Make sure you build her up and treat her with respect. She is the quarter back or point guard of the team. She will show you how to keep it all together. She will coordinate all the other team mates and she will spoil you. If you have one in your life now, be thankful. If not keep your eyes open.

You know the saying, "it's lonely at the top?" That's because they didn't build a team and bring people with them. So if you don't want it to be lonely at the top, do yourself a favor; perfect this step. Make a list of your favorite most productive people, a list of trustworthy people, a list of people who owe you favors, and a list of people who will support you no matter what. If these lists are short, that's okay. We are not looking for quantity; we are looking for quality. Don't fill the list with people you have to motivate and train or coax. Fill the list with people whose skills you can utilize. Again, I urge you to be just as ready and available to help them in return.

Make sure you are thinking in terms of what you need. Don't be greedy but don't be shy either. In my experience, most people are helpful and want to be a part of something big or small. People like to feel needed. Make them a part of your success. Teamwork makes the dream work.

Do you already have some of the teammates in your life? Think about it and write down the name(s) next to the position title. If you do not, give some thought to how you can attract them into your life. Be ready to be a part of their team too. You do not have to go to the person and personally invite them to be on your team unless you want to. That might be a nice touch and they may feel honored. However, there may be some people already committed to you and you just have not noticed.

Fill out the positions with the name of the person or people you think can fill these positions. If you do not have anyone like this in your life, that is okay. You will attract them into your life now.

POSITIONS:

Grandma "Wise Old Soul"

_____

Mama "Cheerleader"

_____

Grandpa "Daddy Warbucks"

_____

Brother "Real World Truth"

_____

Lil Sister "Quarterback"

_____

Now, this is your starting lineup. The rest of the team will be support. Make a list of all the people who you admire, who you think work hard, love hard, make good decisions or whatever you admire about them. What people around you have really gotten your attention with their actions?

    1.
    2.
    3.
    4.
    5.
    6.
    7.

Now make a list of people who admire you. These are people who have your back when you call them. This list may be short and that is okay. It takes a long time to find good people and it is not easy keeping up with them either. Write down the names of the people who like what you do and the way you think. Who speaks highly of you and considers you a good friend or colleague?

1.
2.
3.
4.
5.
6.
7.

Now break down the list. Take each name and give two to three things that stand out about that person. What makes them a good resource? Do they know everybody who is anybody? Are they smarter than you are or they more creative and more organized? What is it about each person you listed above that adds value to your life? As you make the list, keep in mind your weaknesses. You should make a note of areas where you are weak and consider who you know that is strong in that area.

1. _____
2. _____
3. _____
4. _____
5. _____
6. _____
7. _____
8. _____
9. _____
10. _____
11. _____
12. _____
13. _____
14. _____
15. _____

I gave you room for 15 people but if you have more than that, great. Grab another piece of paper and keep writing. If you do not fill all the spaces, that is alright. You will attract the people you need into your life. Right now, just be concerned with figuring out how the people who are already in your life can help you. You should also think about how you can help them. I'm sure they need help too; everyone does.

There should be people that you trust with your life and who trust you with theirs. If you do not have these kinds of people in your life, you need to work on that. Make a decision to choose better friends and be a better friend. Make sure you give to the relationship and make sure you get what you need out of the relationship. Using you resources is the best way to get things done when you are powerless.

Call to action:
1. Review the list of people who owe you favors and people you owe favors to.
2. Identify who from that list can be a resource for you.
3. Make a list of people whose strengths are your weaknesses. List their strengths.
4. Fill out the position list and start to build those relationships if you do not have them.
5. Make a list of people who will help you no matter what you ask

Day 18 – Pep Squad

This chapter may come off a little self-indulgent but who doesn't want their own cheering section? Of course in real life there will not be a set of bleachers with a group of screaming fans following you around everywhere you go, but they should at least be a phone call away.

Now, if you happen to be a performer of any kind, you should always invite people who enjoy your performance so that you will feel comfortable. There is nothing like knowing you are going to get applause at the end to take the pressure off. If however you are not a performer, you may have to round up your applause. You may have to tell the story about your adventure or your accomplishment. If you go back to your resource list, I am sure there are people on it that would enjoy hearing about your success. You have to have a pep squad. Now, I say squad because you need to have more than one to give you the energy and excitement that a sports team gets when they hear the crowd go wild. Have you ever been at a baseball game when a home run is scored or at a basketball game when the star player gets the last shot right at the buzzer? You will have exciting moments just like these and you will need someone to go wild with you.

If you are not a performer or an athlete, you may never have felt that energy before. If you have not, then you really need to feel it now. It may be your children when they see the new car you were able to buy the family. It could be your best friend who helps you celebrate your divorce. It could be a co-worker or client who will toast your promotion. Think about the people who ask you how your day was and really mean it. Do not expect them to spell out your name on a football field but they should at least be able to listen, enjoy the story, and give you praise at the end.

I realized a few years ago how important it is to have people in your corner cheering you on. The road to paradise is not always paved smooth and easy. It can get rough sometimes and when you have a pep squad they keep you going. When you have people not only holding you accountable but getting involved themselves, you are more dedicated to making it through the rough times. When people know their cheers help, they are more likely to be there when you need them. Use the energy to push you forward.

If you get tired and you need a "pick me up," know who you can call for a quick cheer. You may need to rest and your pep squad can reassure you that it is okay to take a break. The pep squad is watching and they can recount your last few weeks of work and remind you of how well you are doing. That way if you take a break, you feel justified. Keep the pep squad close when you do decide to take a break because you may have a hard time going again. If that happens, the pep squad will kick in and get you back on your feet. They will remind you of all the work you put in and tell you to reap the benefits of some of the seeds you have sown. The pep squad will help you push yourself past your limit. The cheers from the crowd will make you run a little faster, play a little harder and stay in the game a little longer.

Right now you will make a list of people who genuinely want to see you succeed. This list will include people who have a vested interest and people who do not. Children can make the best pep squad. If you mentor a child and you tell them your success story, they will brag about your achievement to everyone and try to emulate you. Little children may not have any idea what you have accomplished or what the accomplishment means, they will just match your energy. If you are happy and running around the room, they will join you. If you throw them up in the air in excitement, they will say "do that again. Woo hoo!" So make sure you have at least one child on your list. It does not have to be your child. It has to be a child who you feel comfortable around and who is comfortable around you.

The list you are making is just names of people you can call or go see who will celebrate out loud with you when you are getting close to your goal, when you have reached your goal, or when you are having doubts. You do not have to list any details about them. Just start writing names. List the names of people who will cheer you on to the finish line.

_____

_____

_____

_____

_____

_____

_____

_____

_____

_____

_____

_____

Call to action:

1. List all the people you know who you can call to cheer you on or up when you need it.
2. Start calling them now while you are working your plan.
3. Cheer someone else on their way.

Day 19 – Your Brand

Marketing – Ask yourself," How do people see me?" How do I see myself? Are these things in line? How can I magnify my character so that it becomes my brand? In order to get the most out of the marketing concept, you have to really see yourself for who you are. It's a great thing that we went through the self-evaluation study because it will make it easier for you to define your brand and figure out your target market. Who is your "customer" so to speak? Are you looking for a new career? Are you looking for a mate? Are you ready for a promotion? Do you want to make your children proud? I know you want to make it about you and your journey but right now this chapter is about attracting the things in your life that you want. You have to have a marketing strategy for that.

When you think of marketing I'm sure you think of some big company with major marketing and advertising campaigns. Well good. That's the way you need to think of yourself. You are the CEO of Me, Inc. Everything that McDonalds and Pepsi does is to make you feel a certain way about them. You should do the same. Everything that you do should make people feel a certain way about you. Whether you are doing this consciously or unconsciously, it is what is happening. People feel a certain way about you based on your actions and their perception of those actions. You cannot completely control it but you can assist them in making that decision.

Pepsi cannot make you love their soda but they can give you a feeling about what drinking soda should feel like. They want you to feel like when you drink their soda everything is right in the world, you are happy, enjoying life and you are changing your world. You are with good friends and you are making your dreams come true or something like that. You know what I mean. Whether it is beer, soda, dinner, clothing or a car, the company advertising it wants you to feel a certain way. They want you to feel good, confident and have a need for their product. They want to leave you with your mouth watering, anticipating the experience. I am not telling you to be all things to all people or that you have to please everyone or that the feeling you give them will last forever. Pick a target market the same way Pepsi did. Whether your goal is to excite your spouse, your children, your employees or your next boyfriend, do the things that will get their attention. The idea is that you put out what you want people to know about you or feel about you. They do not have to like it. The same way you see a product, make a decision about it, and buy it or pass it over. Your goal is to show the world who you are and they can make the choice to partake or to move on. You are not asking for approval. So remember, marketing is about a feeling. What do you want people to feel when they see you or when they talk about you?

You should always be on purpose. Be yourself and be sure who that is; no pretending. McDonalds is not trying to be Burger King. Pepsi is not trying to be Coke. They have found their place and they are amplifying that place. Find your place. McDonalds is fried and Burger King is flame broiled. BMW is a performance vehicle; the ultimate driving machine and Mercedes is about the luxury ride. Do you see how they have set themselves apart from their competition?

Right now I want you to think of a life mission. Write down two or three possibilities of what you want to do in life. Not career wise, but personally. Now of course you can turn it into a career but first, find it and work it in your everyday life. What is it?

Write down your thoughts:

_____
_____
_____
_____
_____
_____
_____

_____

_____

_____

Here is an example of a mission statement: *I want to be known as a person who knows how to get what she wants and can help others get what they want. I want people to know I care about their goals.* Pick something that is natural to you. This way you will stick to your mission easily just being yourself; the "you" that you are committed to becoming. When you think of your mission statement, it has to be something that is actionable, measurable and something that you can maintain. I will show you what I mean by breaking down the mission statement example. Actionable: When someone has a problem, assist them in finding a solution. When I want something have a list of people or places I can go to get it. Measurable: Count the number of people you have helped. This is how you can tell if you are living the mission statement. What is your niche? Think about it for a minute. What is it that makes you special? Is there something that you really like to accomplish by the end of the day? Your mission is about what makes you feel proud. When you leave the room do you want people to say you were nice, you were funny, you were smart? What actions do you want to take? You can be the most caring, the funniest, the most fashionable or the best mother. Take a second to think about what you would like your claim to fame to be and write it down.

_____

_____

_____

_____

In the rare event that you could not figure out what you leave behind, here is your chance to decide for yourself what characteristic you would like others to remember about you. Now let's move on to what to do with it. First thing you do, is turn it into your personal mission statement. Write out the mission statement and read it out loud.

_____

_____

_____

_____

Turn it into your personal marketing campaign. Let us use our earlier example. If you are good at helping people and you want them to remember you that way, find out what they want out of life, this year, or tonight and offer to help them find it. Give suggestions if you already know something that will help them. End the conversation by saying, "call me if you need help finding that." Or you could say, "I know someone you should meet; they have just what you are looking for." You should always be interested in people's stories. Listening should be a way of life for you so you can hear what they want. You should also be good at communicating quickly how they can benefit from the information you are going to give them. When someone asks you for help, you should do it with great joy. You shouldn't complain. This should make your day. Word should get around that you are helpful and that if someone needs something they should call you. You should be pleasant and easily accessible. This strategy will help you reach your mission. You will have the reputation that you are helpful and people who you have helped will tell their stories about you. You are a go-getter and people should come to you when they can't figure out how to get what they want.

Your mission statement and marketing campaign are basically your reputation. When you have made a reputation for yourself that matches your mission statement you know that you are successful.

When you speak of your mission, you should be passionate. What characteristics should you possess to achieve your persona? If you are not already this way, do not worry; you can change. You can become whomever you want. All you have to do is commit to it. Start acting and reacting the way you want to be known. Live your life this way every day and before you know it, you will have reached your mission.

I have a friend who was always told he was mean. He was a mean kid, a mean teenager and finally ended up being a mean man. He hated hearing it. One day he was talking to a group of people and they were wondering where this one person was whom they had not seen in a while. Everyone agreed that this person was so nice. The whole day, he watched as they asked each person they saw who knew this man, if they had seen him lately and everyone would reply, "No, I haven't seen him lately but I wish I had. He was so nice." He started to wish he had met the man. What was so nice about him? He began to wonder, "If I went away would people agree that

I was nice?" He doubted it. He didn't know why people thought he was so mean but that was not the way he wanted to be seen.

He wanted to be nice. So at that moment, he decided he would be nice. Believe it or not it worked. He didn't say mean things anymore; he thought about his words before he spoke. He knew it wasn't always what he said but how he said it. He was more patient with people. He would give them a chance to express themselves and make mistakes without judging them. He didn't complain as much and he learned to compliment people when they did something good. These small changes changed the way people viewed him. Now when asked, people say he is nice. That was a conscious decision to create his marketing strategy. For others, it may just kind of happen. Either way, you need to embrace it once you realize it.

Marketing tells people how to feel about you. What is the first and last thing you want people to think about when you leave the room or when you enter a room? When you walk in a room and someone you know is there, what should pop into their head and their heart about you? When you leave, what should they miss about you? When you are not around, what thoughts should remind them of you? When you find your niche and market it, you will feel more confident in your everyday life.

Call to action:
1. Find your niche; what makes you special?
2. Write your missions statement.
3. Begin living it daily.

Day 20 – Reward Yourself

Today you need to remind yourself of all the things you have done so far. Go back and read your accomplishments from the past and add to that list some of the things you have done so far. Today your task is to go to the table of contents and look at the list of chapters you have already completed (1-19) and pick one to re-read. After you re-read it, if some of your answers have changed, make a note of them. Do not cross them out because you will see your progress when you come back to the chapter again. After you have re-read the chapter, it is time for you to do something fun, rewarding and totally about you. Go to the list of things you like or the bucket list and pull out something that will make you feel good.

Today is about celebrating your successes however big or small. Make a list or recall in your mind what you want to celebrate. Go to the store and buy yourself a greeting card. Inside write a short thank you or note of appreciation. Tell yourself how you have enjoyed the work so far or whatever you feel. The card is a way to verbally and physically express your gratitude. If you want to put the card on your desk, night stand or cocktail table, go ahead. If you want to keep it to yourself, put it in your gym bag, purse or briefcase. If people ask you about it, you have the choice to tell them what you have been working on or to just smile and say what comes to mind. Keep it a secret or tell the world. It is your choice.

Not everyone will understand what you are doing. Some people will once you explain it, but others may never get it. When we do not understand something, we tend to take the negative and talk down about it. Please do not give someone like this power over you. Let them know you appreciate them sharing but you know what you are doing and you are happy. If the person is your significant other, you would like to have their blessing but you may not, so let your example be your testimony. They will believe it when they see it.

_____
_____
_____
_____
_____
_____
_____
_____
_____
_____
_____
_____
_____
_____
_____
_____
_____

Call to action:
1. Do something you like or something on your bucket list.
2. Write down your reflection of the last few weeks.
3. Read your past accomplishments and add any new ones.
4. Choose a chapter to re-read.

Day 21 – Letter for help

Before you start to read this chapter, I need you to commit to having an open mind. Some of the things we will discuss may be foreign to you. You may have heard of them but you may not have tried them before. I want you to be open while you are reading this, doing the exercise and utilizing this principle in your life. Remember, all of these principals are optional. You do not have to do any of this. You can continue doing things the way you have been and your starting over experience will take your life back to the same way it was. Have you heard the saying if you want a different result you have to do something different? That may not be exactly the way it was said but you get what I am saying. Getting out of your comfort zone and making yourself do things with your life that you have not done before, can take you to places you have never been.

The first time I did this exercise, I surprised myself at how many of the things in my letter had been fulfilled. I was young and my mind was not open but I was obedient so I tried it. It helped me think clearly about what I wanted. It helped me figure out who could help me and made me more committed to the goals I set. I know it will do the same for you if you do it wholeheartedly.

Right now you have been working on this starting over process for at least 20 days. Some of you may have put it down and come back to it but you have done 20 exercises before this one. You either feel it working already in your life or you can see how it will work in your life soon. Keep going. This is an important part of the process.

Do you remember some of the things we talked about earlier? Go back in the book and remind yourself of the work you have done. You set goals and tasks to get you moving. You wrote down the people who can help you. You discovered more about yourself by self evaluation and you have rewarded yourself twice. Did you deserve that reward? Yes, you did. Think about any changes that you have experienced in the last few weeks. Have your actions or reactions changed at all? Have you changed your daily activity? Have you found yourself being nicer or sterner with the people in your life? Think about what you are experiencing.

Let yourself get emotional. If it makes you sad that you did not do this earlier, that is okay. You are allowed to feel whatever you are feeling. Do not stop yourself and do not coach yourself. Whatever feelings are forming inside of you let them form. What is it about your life that you want to change? What do you want to get rid of and what do you want more of? That is what I really want you to think about right now. You have been feeling like you want to let go of some things. You may have some people, situations or things in your life that you just do not want to deal with anymore. Some of those things may be difficult to part from. This exercise is not to get rid of people, places or things. This exercise is to get rid of the feeling or reaction you get from those things. However, sometimes it is necessary to let go of the person, place or thing in order to get rid of the feeling. For now, focus on the feeling. Write a list of feelings and reactions you would like to remove from your life. Be careful not to put people, places or things on the list.

If your child is stressing you out do not say you want your son out of your life, instead say you want your son to stop getting into trouble and making you feel like a bad parent. You do not want to feel embarrassed about your daughter's behavior anymore. You do not want to feel responsible for your son. You want to feel less stress or the freedom to say "no" to your daughter. It is the feeling or reaction you really do not want. So focus there and begin your list now. Take as long as you want and write as much as you like. Allow yourself to feel some of those negative emotions so that you can remember them and get rid of them. Feel the hurt, the stress, the fear, or whatever drags you down. Let it all out. Release what is holding you back. Start writing here and continue on another sheet if you need to.

Read over the list again. On a separate sheet of paper list the feelings you want to remove from your life using one word descriptions. Write down things like; lack, stress, pressure, fear, judgment, gossip or whatever you want to get rid of. Now in a safe manner, burn the paper. Burn away all the negative things that are holding you hostage to your unhappiness.

Now that you are clear on what you do not want in your life, it is time to get clarity on the things you do want in your life. In this exercise, I do not want you to list people, places or things. I want you to focus on the feelings. For example, do not say I want a husband, a new car, or a shopping spree. For instance, the husband represents love, companionship and support. The shopping spree may help you to feel pretty or wealthy or giving. The new car gives you perfect transportation. You may never have to count on anyone else or worry about a break down if you have a new car.

Write as many feelings as you like; nobody is stopping you or judging you. Whatever you want in your life, write it down. Even if you never really felt it before but you think you want to feel it, write it down. Even if you think you do not deserve it, write it down. You do not have to know how these things are going to come into your life to write them down, you only need to know that you want them in your life. Writing it down will help attract it into your life. This book is about being aware. When you are aware, you can make informed decisions. The decisions you make affect your daily life. The decision to read this book will affect your life and doing these exercises with an open mind will affect your life as well. Begin writing down all the feelings you can think of that you want in your life.

1.
2.
3.
4.
5.
6.
7.
8.
9.
10.
11.
12.
13.

14.

15.

16.

17.

18.

19.

20.

21.

22.

23.

24.

25.

Great! Now you know what you want in your life and you can verbalize it when asked. In the next few weeks, you will be asked "how can I help" or "what can I do for you." And you will have an answer. Look at your list. Or you will see an opportunity and you will know that it is yours because you wrote it down here. When you are asked, "how can I help you," go directly to this book and find a feeling from this list, or a need from the previous list, or a task you need to delegate that you know this person can definitely assist with. Whatever you do, do not answer "I don't know" because you do know. You wrote it down. If you cannot recall your list say, "let me get back to you." Then make sure you get back to them. Do not block your blessings. Be open to help and be ready when you get an offer. Opportunity should not have to knock; you should be standing there waiting with the door open. Greet opportunity with a smile because you know what you want and you are prepared to receive it.

Have you ever written a letter to Santa? Sure it was a very long time ago if you did. But can you remember how you felt after you wrote the letter? You may have felt like you were surely going to get what you wanted for Christmas because now Santa knew exactly what to bring. If you did not write a letter, maybe you went to sit on Santa's lap. You told Santa what you wanted for Christmas and when that day came you were excited to know that all you had to do was ask and you would get it. Well that has not changed. All you have to do is ask and you will get it.

As we discussed before, you have to know what you want so that you can ask. So now that you know, it is time for you to ask. You may not believe in Santa anymore but you have some other beliefs. They may be religious, spiritual or something personal that you concluded in your life experiences. Whatever it is, it is time to tap into it. I want you to write a letter to whatever or whoever you believe in. You can address it however you like. You may say Dear God, Dear Universe, Dear Kiné (insert your name) or whoever makes you feel like you did when you wrote the letter to Santa. You decide who can help you get what you want and write to them. They are ready to listen; you just have to write it down.

Add in all the things you wrote in your list above and the things you wrote earlier in this book. If you want a great relationship, then say that. If you want an honest business partner, say that. Whatever you want, ask for it. Do not hold back. Let the world know what to send you. One little piece of advice: try not to use the word want. What will happen is, you will create more want and you do not want that. In place of the word "want," reword the sentence as if you already have it. So for example, if your sentence was going to be "I want enough money to take care of my family", change the sentence to – "I have more than enough money to take care of my family". That is what makes this letter different than your original letter to Santa. You are not requesting these things, you are attracting these things. They are so close and all you have to do is get close enough to them so you can grab them. Attract your dreams to you the same way you attract the opposite sex to you. Dress right, smell right, look right and present yourself right.

Write the letter with the passion you would write to someone you were in love with. The emotion needs to jump off the page. All the words are yours but there is one thing you have to put in this letter. At the end, you have to say thank you for giving me everything I asked for. You have to say it and mean it. "Thank you for giving me everything I asked for." You can use the space to start your letter. You may consider it a first draft and want to rewrite it or add to it. Just start writing and as you write, you will become more and more open.

Dear _____,

_____
_____
_____
_____
_____
_____
_____
_____
_____
_____
_____
_____
_____
_____
_____
_____
_____
_____
_____
_____
_____
_____
_____
_____
_____
_____
_____
_____
_____
_____
_____

Did you remember to say thank you at the end? Now go forth in the same
manner you wrote the letter. Act as if you already have it or if it is easier
for you, act as if you are going to get it right now.

The next thing I want you to do is to tell the universe that you are open to all blessings. Energy is always flowing and part of that energy is yours. However, if you are sitting back blocking your blessings, someone else may be receiving your energy. Tear down your energy blocks and let all your blessings flow to you. Say out loud, "Universe if there is a blessing out there for me, please give it to me. I accept it with great gratitude." You can say this everyday or ten times a day if you want. Do not be afraid to ask and do not be afraid to receive.

Call to action:

1. Write a list of things you want to get out of your life.
2. Write a list of things you want more of in your life.
3. Write a letter asking for the things you want.
4. Recite your request to the universe daily.

Day 22 – Activity Sheet

In order to have the most productive day, week, month and year, you need to plan. This chapter is a serious planning chapter. If this was a business plan, this chapter would describe your strategy. How do you plan to make the changes you want to make in your life? You already wrote down your goals and a list of tasks that would help you get your goals accomplished. Now you have to break your tasks down into activities. Some of these activities will be consistent and need to happen on a daily or weekly basis, while others may only happen once a week or every once in a while. I will give you an example of an activity sheet. You can feel free to use it or you can make or find your own. Do what makes you comfortable. Do not however, use this as an excuse not to get started. If you do not have an activity sheet, use this one until you think of something else. You have done enough thinking, feeling and writing. This exercise will help you put those thoughts, words and feelings into action.

Take a look at your task list and start to prioritize the tasks. Assign them to days first. Later, we will give them time slots. Make sure that you get the task done on time if you have deadlines. Missed deadlines could mean missed opportunities.

What are you going to do each day?

Monday	
Example: *go to the gym*	

Tuesday	
Example: *check P.O. Box*	

Wednesday	
Example: *get hair cut*	

Thursday	
Example: *Get car washed*	

Friday	
Example: *Take Children to movie*	

Saturday	
Example: *Date night*	

Sunday	
Example: *go to church*	

The next thing you are going to do, block off time on the activity sheet to get each task done. First take a pencil and shade off all the times that are already spoken for. There are tasks in your life right now that you need to do like pick up the kids from school, fix dinner, watch your favorite TV show, go to church, or go to the gym. Shade in those areas now. Next, find a time slot for all the new tasks you have. Make sure you are kind enough to yourself to pick a time that works best. It is your schedule so make it easy to follow. You know your strengths and weaknesses so remember them and lean toward your strengths. If you have more energy in the morning, put the more difficult things in the morning. If your energy is low in the evening, schedule things in the evening that are easier to do or that energize you. Do not start early in the morning if you are not a morning person. You will be setting yourself up for failure. On the contrary, if you are not good at night do not schedule things too late. It is not good to fail so set up your schedule in a way that makes you a successful person.

Time	Sunday	Monday	Tuesday	Wednesday	Thursday	Friday	Saturday
6am							
7							
8							
9							
10							
11							
12pm							
1							
2							
3							
4							
5							
6							
7							
8							
9							
10							
11							
12am							
1							
2							
3							
4							
5am							

This is your schedule so you make it work for you. As I said before, there are some things that happen that you cannot control the times for like school, church and work. For all other things, make them happen at your convenience. This will help you get the most out of your schedule and it will help you accomplish your goals. Also remember to use the schedule, especially on days that are busy. You do not want to forget important events and activities. If you do not take the time to look at the schedule, filling it out is pointless.

Many people think of schedules as restrictive. You may want to change your perspective on that if you are one of those people. Schedules can be freeing. They can keep you from making costly mistakes that stress you out. You can cut down on over-booking or over committing yourself. It can also help you get more done because you have a realistic view of your day and what all you need to accomplish. If you find you have a free day or a light day, first check your task list to see if you have any deadlines coming up. If you are on schedule, then let the day remain light. If you see that you are falling behind, fill the day with activity.

You do not have to tire yourself out. Some people think if they are tired that means they were productive. Productivity is when you are making the things you need to do, the things you have done. When you are able to scratch items off of your "to do" list, you are productive. At the beginning of everyday you should have a "to do" list. I personally make my "to do" list the night before so that I am not thinking all night about what I need to do tomorrow and what I did not get done today. This helps me sleep better. Your "To Do" list should have things that do not happen on a daily or weekly basis. This may be returning a specific person's phone call or going to the store to buy a certain item. You can fill your schedule with items from your "to do" list at various times or you can block off time to conquer the list.

Another way is to work on your task with like tasks. If you know you have five or six phone calls to make, you can make them all at a set time. If phone calls are part of your daily activity anyway, you can do it then. While we are on the subject of phone calls, be mindful of incoming calls. It is okay to take calls as long as you stay on task. Let the person know you were in the middle of something but you will take a few minutes for them. Do not let them control your day. You can tell them I will give you a call back at a time when I can give you my full attention. It is not mean, it is necessary to get things done. If you want to converse with your friends, find things to do together so you can all make money, have fun or talk as long as they like. You need personal time; moments when you just talk and chill. Brace yourself for this. You can have all that; you just need to schedule it in or take it when you see a natural break. Do not do it during the times you should be productive. Successful people get stuff done. They do not wait for things to happen; they make them happen. Successful people understand that time is money.

Being on time and doing things in a timely manner aid in your success. If you are late, you are disrespectful. You disrespect yourself, your business and the person you are meeting with. You leave a bad impression when you are late. It sends a message that you do not care or that you think you are more important than the other person. People get angry or resentful when you waste their time. Your time should be important to you and you should respect other's time as well. The more time you waste, the harder you will have to work to make it up. When you do things in a timely manner (meaning just get them done,) you will have time to chill or do more work if you choose.

One of the things that people do to waste time the most is procrastinate. My motto has always been "why put off until tomorrow what you can do today?" Procrastinators on the other hand, say "why do today what you can put off until tomorrow?" Some of their favorite words are someday, one day and soon. What if someday came five days ago? You cannot be ready for opportunity when it knocks if you are waiting on one day to come or if you are going to take care of your business soon. Soon is not a time. I am not telling you to rush; I am simply saying stay diligent and dedicated to your goals. If you want things to happen in your life, you have to take action. When you put off tasks and activities that get you closer to your goal, you literally push your goal further away. You also miss opportunities that the universe set up in your favor. Now that you have made this activity sheet, begin using it. Change it when you need to in order to be more productive. It is your schedule and activity sheet, so make it work for you.

Call to action:
1. List your daily tasks using the task list you created.
2. Assign times to each task using the activity sheet.
3. Practice being on time.

4. Practice taking control of your time and letting people know you will get back to them.
5. Make a "to do" list daily and scratch off tasks as you complete them.
6. Use the activity sheet weekly so that you can track your habits and progress.

Day 23 – Delegate

Everything that has to get done does not have to get done by you. Delegating is about using your resources. When you delegate, you free up time for yourself to do the things that can truly only be done by you. Sometimes you *are* the only person who knows how to do something or it may simply be your job or you are the best person to handle it. When this is the case, those are the things that really can only get done by you. Do those things and delegate as many of the other ones as you can. Earlier, you made a list of people and resources you have in your life. You also made a list of needs and people who could fill those needs. Now it is time to put that list to work for you. Delegating is an essential part of success. Successful people hire the right people. They do not give themselves legal advice or prepare their own taxes or do their laundry. When you are changing your life, giving up control in certain areas can be a big help. It is not going to be easy if you feel that you have to have control over everything. But once you get use to it, you will love having one less thing on your list of things to do. Put some of your things on someone else's list and watch them get done rather than doing them yourself.

This is the time when you really start to move to a different place in life. Take a look at your task list, "to do" list, and daily activity sheet. Then make a new list of things that you can delegate. Doctors appointments, playing with your children, meeting clients or going to work has to get done by you. There are things like filing, cooking, picking kids up from school, checking emails and voicemails that someone else can do. What things can you hire someone for or just delegate to a friend, family member or co-worker? You may not be able to hire someone right now but do not think about *how* at this point. Your job right now is to think about *what*. The idea is to identify the things you can delegate. Later, we will figure out when the time is right.

The best thing for you to do right now is to make a list of all the things that you do on a daily basis that you can delegate. Do not start thinking about who will do them or how well they will get them done. Just write down what you are able to delegate. Be honest with yourself. I am not suggesting that every task will get delegated. I just want you to be aware of what can be delegated and especially of what you wish you could delegate. This way, you identify the things that really do <u>have</u> to get done by you.

Below, write a list of things you can, would, should, wish or think about delegating. Make the list as long as you like; it is your wish list. If you think of something else later, come back and write it down.

Example: walking the dog, getting car washed, repairing the sink

_____
_____
_____
_____

There are things that you do that probably were not on your activity sheet like grocery shopping, laundry, watching television or cleaning up. These things can be delegated also. You can record your television shows and watch them at a time that is more convenient for you instead of when they are scheduled to air on television. You can hire someone to do the other things if you can afford it or you can barter with someone. If you have older children, you should give them chores to help relieve some of the pressure. They may not get done perfectly, but it is easier for you to go behind them and tighten up something, than starting from scratch?

Now to the control freaks, delegating is going to be difficult because you believe that everything is better if you do it. That is not always true. There are times that we ruin things because we could not give up control. Unfortunately, this chapter will not completely cure the control freak in you, but it will allow you to start identifying and accepting that you are obsessed with control. You can begin working on it today and if you are committed, you will cure yourself and enjoy a life of assistance. Some of the things in this book will help you realize that you cannot do it alone. You will realize that you need assistance and that just because you do it well, does not mean someone else cannot do it well also. Who said your way is the right way anyway? I was a control freak and sometimes I revert back to my wicked ways and have to coach myself out of it because I know that behavior does not benefit me in the long run. Being a control freak is stressful and it makes your life harder, not easier. So if this is you, start preparing your mind to let go.

The truth is you really are not in control anyway. Your feeling of control is an illusion you have taught yourself that makes you feel comfortable. Nobody really has external control. You cannot control what other people do. The only thing you can really control is how you react to situations. You can go crazy, you can remain calm, you can go into deep thought or you can give up. Teaching yourself how to control your emotions and reactions is a better way to spend your time rather than trying to control external things in the world that you will never really control.

The next step is to take the wish list you started and begin assigning the list away. Now, you do have to be realistic. Do not delegate a task to someone who is incapable of getting it done. If you are thinking of hiring a person or a company to take on a task and you cannot afford it right now, write it down on your goal list. Then set a goal that will allow you to be in a position to hire someone.

Below, you are going to re-write your list. Except this time, write down next to the task you are delegating, who will take that task from you.

Task	Task Master

Your list is down and you know who can handle the jobs. From here, you have to ask them to take on the task. Hopefully you are utilizing people from your resource list. Choose people who naturally want to support you or people who are good at helping others. This way they will take on the task with open arms. There are times when you will have to force, beg or insist that the person help you, so do not be afraid when that happens. You may have teenage children who just like to complain every chance they get, but let them do their complaining and help them understand how their help is a part of the big picture. You may need to get child support from your children's father or apply for unemployment or other government assistance while you start your business or look for a new job. Maybe you have a co-worker who is not doing their fair share and you have been doing a job that clearly belongs to them. Teach them what you do and pass the job back over to them.

Whatever you need to do to get some harmony in your life, do it now. When you learn to delegate, you feel a lot less stress and you are more mentally and physically free to pursue your goals. You can start out slow and work your way up this list. Do what makes you comfortable but do not "chicken out" and put it back on your list. If you do not have someone already in your life that can handle a delegated task, make sure you are aware when they come into your life. Blessings and opportunities come into our lives daily; we just have to recognize them and say thank you so that they can continue to flow. Tell the universe what you need and you will get it.

Keep in mind the reason you are delegating. We may not have it all together, but together we can have it all. Teamwork makes the dream work. Build your team and work toward the greater good. Help others and allow them to help you. Stay focused, ask for help when you need it, and always do your best. Delegate yourself to a stress free life.

Call to action:
1. Write down your list of tasks you wish to delegate.
2. Write down who will take on the delegated task.
3. Take a task off of someone else's list. Help them delegate.

Day 24 – Technology

Technology is one of those bitter sweet things. At times you wonder why we have so much, and at other times you wonder how you ever lived without it. Do you indulge in all the technological advancements or are you a technophobe? Are you putting systems in place to simplify your life or do you like to keep it old school? Are you still rewinding VHS videos and checking your answering machine (not voicemail)? Don't be scared of technology. It can help you make life easier and take it to the next level. Many times people make excuses for why they do not like technology and the truth is they are not being honest with themselves. Do not lie to yourself. If something can help you simplify your life, do not be afraid to use it. If you are afraid, just say you do not like it because you do not know how to use it and ask for help.

Usually the children in our lives can learn the new tech products without even reading the direction so ask them to help you. Who cares how you learn it; that does not matter. Just get it. Before she passed away in 2011, my 85 year old grandmother had a Facebook page and emailed me updates on entertainment news and recipes. She loved it. I know you are still fussing about how much time it takes to learn something new and how different it is from the way it used to be. Well I'll name a few things that changed our way of life and you tell me if you want to leave without them.

For example: would you go back to reading by candle light? I don't think so. Would you like to dip your pen in ink to write or do you like it the way it is now? What about your telephone or even better your cell phone?

How do you enjoying being able to call your children whenever you want and they better answer; no excuses, right? How about the drive-through or the fast food restaurant period? And the indoor toilet, how do you feel about that handy dandy technological advancement? Do you want to dig a hole out back or will you keep your Porcelain God?

Let's face it; there are things that just make life easier and sometimes more enjoyable. Do not deny it and do not miss out on it. I can understand if you are against one advancement or another because you believe it will have an adverse effect on the earth. Many innovations will and do. If you want to stand your ground and refrain from using it, you do that. You have to stick to your beliefs. However, if your main concern is price, just wait until it goes on sale. They always start out astronomically priced and then end up practically free within a year. Or if you just do not want to learn something new, stop being lazy and enjoy the future. Ok; I am done fussing. I think you get the point so let's move on.

So, if you have a business and you are struggling with some of the processes, you should adopt a better system. Find one that will streamline the process and cut out a few steps. Sometimes you can also cut out a few people. If that means someone loses a job that is sad so I understand your hesitation. However, my darling, that is a part of decision making. You cannot always make emotional decisions; you have to use logic and do what is most cost effective. You have to make tough and painful decisions that are not always nice. Sometimes that decision can be between losing the business or losing an employee?

These days there are systems and software created to simplify solutions for small, medium and large businesses. All of them will not be right for you but check and see what is out there that can make your business and personal life run smoother. If nothing else, it is essential to have a computer or tablet, an internet connection and a cell phone. If you do not have these things you are missing out on a lifestyle that can be more peaceful.

Do you miss seeing family or friends? Well these days you can call them using small video cameras that connect to your computer and it can be free or very inexpensive. Yes, talk over the phone using your computer and see real time video of the person you are talking to. You can also use your cell phone. That is just the beginning of the advancements there are so many more and there are more coming. I am about to tell you a story and I want

126 | Kiné Corder

you to count the number of technological instruments mentioned. I only want you to count the ones that have become big in the last 20 years. So do not count toilets, lights, cars and record players; count stuff like fax machines, cell phones, airbags and blue tooth devices. I also want you to count the ones that you own or use.

Daniel is a 29 year old who hated his life. He complained about it to everyone who would listen. After a while, people stopped wanting him to come around. They stopped inviting him places and he became depressed. With no social life he decided to go to college and finish that degree he never received. He enrolled in an online bachelor degree program and finished in 2 years. He was so proud of himself. He sent out an email blast to inform all his friends of his accomplishment. A few of his friends were so happy for him that they started calling him again. He had 12 messages on his cell phone voicemail when he awakened the next afternoon.

His parents however, didn't believe him. They needed proof. So he Skyped them and put his degree in front of the camera so they could see it over video. His mother began to cry. They could not believe their prayers were answered and their baby had finally finished something. The mother immediately went on the internet and booked a flight for her son to come home and visit. Well, because it was a surprise, she did not ask Daniel if his schedule conflicted. Turns out, he had a meeting booked in the middle of the trip but he was so excited and thankful that he told his mother he would work something out. Daniel called his clients and told them that he would have to change their face to face meeting to a web conference call. The clients loved the idea because they did not want to drive through traffic anyway.

A few days later, Daniel was in his parents' house looking at his old room. He took out his cell phone and took a picture of the old trophies and pictures on the walls. He then sent his brother a text message with the pictures attached. He also posted the picture on his Facebook page. He posted, "I am back and better than ever." His best friend Matt from high school saw it and realized Dan was in town so he dropped by. They talked about what was happening in each other's lives and Matt pulled out his digital camera and showed Dan pictures of his two children and his wife.

They decided to Google another old friend and see if they could find something on him. Apparently, he had broken the law and not only was there articles written about him, he was also on the correctional website and a "girl do not date him" website. "Wow", they thought. "And we thought our lives were bad." Dan grabbed a few beers and some bottled waters for them and they sat on the porch talking for several hours more.

Later that week, Dan had a conference call and a webcast. He was able to turn two prospects into clients and up sold one of his current clients. Can you believe he took three credit card payments over the phone and in 2-3 business days the money was in his business bank account? This allowed him to stay at home a few days longer. That was just enough time for him to get the courage up to go see that teacher who had high hopes for him. Mrs. Tanner was still teaching, well, tutoring part-time at the high school. Dan walked in and told her all about what he had been doing. She told him she had a LinkedIn page and if he got connected with her, she would send him referrals.

He left the school with a smile on his face and left the city with an even bigger smile. Dan was now running a little late for his flight because he had stayed in Mrs. Tanner's office too long. While he was on the shuttle to the airport, he checked in for his flight using mobile check in on his cell phone. Because he did not have to check any bags, he went straight to the gate and actually had time to spare. While waiting in the airport, Daniel logged onto the internet on his laptop. He didn't have to use his wireless connection because the airport had free wifi. He was having such a good time that he had never checked on his house. He was able to log onto his alarm system and check on his valuables at home right from the airport. Everything was the way he left it. So he felt peaceful. Not just because he could see his house from hundreds of miles away, but because he realized for the first time in a long time that he was successful.

He did not have a million dollars but he had some hopes, dreams, goals and a clear plan to get there. He had most of the things he wanted and he had made his mother proud. Above all, he was now satisfied with his life and whatever great things he would do from here on out would be gravy to the full life he was already living. He just needed to change a few things, adjust his perspective and keep moving forward.

Count the number of times Daniel used technology? _____ How many of those do you use yourself? _____

Technology gave Daniel a chance to experience life and view life in a different way. How can you be like Daniel?

List the types of technological advancements that you could utilize in your personal and business life to make your life, your clients' lives, or the lives of the people around you, much powerful, peaceful or pleasurable.

_____

_____

_____

_____

_____

_____

_____

_____

Call to action:
1. Count up all the uses of technology in the story.
2. Determine what new technology you can utilize to make your life easier.
3. Make a plan to purchase technology and implement these things in your life.

(The answer is 23 uses of technology)

Day 25 – Cut Cost

How many times have you bought things that you really did not need but they seemed like a good idea at the time? Have you ever paid a late fee or an over-draft fee? Do you put everyday purchases on credit cards? The biggest question is, are you living outside your means?

Are you trying to keep up with the Joneses or are you trying to be the Joneses? Let me break some news to you, the Joneses do not exist. Everyone is trying to keep up with some imaginary idea. The Joneses are living outside of their means too. They are barely holding it together but nobody can see what they are going through because they hide it with jewelry, cars and clothes. They make sure you do not see them struggle because in actuality they are trying to keep up with you.

We are all so silly. We stress ourselves out because we do not want anyone to know that we cannot afford something or that we cannot make all our monthly payments. No matter how much money you make, whether it is $50,000 a year or $50 million, you are still broke if you are spending more than you make. Bankrupt is bankrupt. Making more money does not change your money habits. But you have to do it if you want peace in your life.

A long time ago, way back when you got your first allowance or maybe even before, you adopted an idea about money. It may have come from what your parents were doing with their money or what they were not doing. It may have come from having a lot or barely having anything. It could have come from how the people around you described money or it simply from the little knowledge you had of money.

I am not assuming that everyone reading this is broke. There are some people who have been great stewards over their money. They are not keeping up with the Joneses, they are not trying to be the Joneses, and they are happy with their financial situation. Some of you may have had a hardship, a medical issue or a tough break that brought you down. Whether you are making a choice to start over or you had a life change like a job layoff or divorce you should still work to cut cost during this transition.

Either way, there have to be some changes in your finances starting today. If your income has decreased, then your expenses have to decrease as well. This is hard because it causes us to make sacrifices and to give up things we like. I encourage people to seek the maximum pleasure out of life so I am not going to tell you to give up all the things you love that are expensive. What I will say is, do things in moderation and plan your purchases. When you follow those two rules you are able to live an abundant life without feeling like you are restricted. Being poor or broke is not about how much money you make but about how much you keep. If you cannot afford to do what you want to do because you are over extended or your money is tied up, basically you are broke. Just be honest with yourself.

Making a budget or spending plan is really not a bad thing. When you make a spending plan, you give yourself limitations that keep you in line and allow you to really be wealthy. Set a spending plan that gives you the leeway to live the life you want without creating the stressful moments you do not want.

A spending plan should include all the things you spend money on. The key word is ALL. You want to list everything because you want to make sure you have enough money for everything.

The first thing you want to do is list all of your income. Add up your pay check, your business income, your child support, government assistance, gifts, investments, alimony and any other ways you make money. The next thing you do is list all the things you spend money on. The way you do this is to look at your past spending habits. If you use your debit card, go back and look at your last two bank statements. If you just get money out of the ATM and spend it, this may be a little harder for you. It is hard to remember everything you spent money on once it is gone. If you usually spend cash, you need to track your spending for the next few days and try to recall your habits and begin writing them all down. Figure out where your money goes.

If you do not use a budget, one can be provided for you. Just go to www.kinecorder.com/spendingplan where you can download a budget I use myself and my financial planning clients. If you already have a budget, go ahead and use it if it works for you. The reason I like the spending plan I created is because it separates expenses into fixed expenses like mortgage and insurance, variable expenses like bills that fluctuate or things you do not have to do every month, and luxury expenses like entertainment. This allows you to see what you need to cut. The luxury expenses are the first to go if you need to cut anything out of your monthly budget.

Once you have calculated all your income, tracked your spending, and filled in the items on the budget, go back and find places where you can cut expenses by either deleting them, decreasing the frequency in which you purchase them or decreasing the quantity you purchase. Some people like to buy generic or an off brand. That may work to lower the cost. Another good idea is to stay out of the store. Try to buy everything you need at once. The more you go to the store, the more likely you are to over spend. Also, plan your purchases. If you are looking to buy a new TV, do not do it on impulse while you are in the store and spend top dollar. Wait for the product to go on sale to purchase it.

Most of the retail items we buy are ridiculously overpriced. Depending on the industry, the product could be marked up anywhere 500% or more. Something that costs $ .60 cents to make in Taiwan is on retail for $25.00 in America. We buy it because we do not know any better. Also, prices are manmade so they are negotiable. Do not be unreasonable but always find out if there are discounts that are not published or that the manager or owner is willing to give.

Getting back to that budget, when you are planning your money, you need to determine early on how much you are prepared to spend in each area. There are necessities and there are luxuries. You should not even look at the luxuries until you have completely taken care of the necessities. I know this is easier said than done because we have a hard time identifying our luxuries. We think of every purchase as a necessity. Smoking, going out to eat, alcohol, and the gym membership are all luxuries. But these are things that we consume on a daily basis and they have become needs instead of wants.

Below are different financial planning ideas. They really are the same thing but some people like to break down their expenses into categories more than others. I have used them myself at different times in my life. You can decide which one works best for you and your family's situation.

The first one is a 10, 10, 80 plan. This means that 10% should go toward giving, 10% toward saving and investing and 80% of your money should go toward living expenses. Everything on that budget except for giving and saving should be included in that 80%. This even includes debt repayment. This is not a bad way to live if you can keep yourself focused. If you receive a pay check every two weeks from your job you may enjoy this method and find it easy to follow. Go ahead and have your 401K taken out before taxes. If your company matches, allocate the amount they match. The rest you can take out and save in another financial institution. It gets tricky however when you are self-employed. You do not make the same amount of money every month so it can be difficult to budget and it is hard to find a personal finance book written with good ideas for the self-employed. Budget on the worst case scenario; use the amount of money you would make on your worst week. If you make more money one week or another leave it in the bank, do not spend it. Continue to live modestly because you do not know when you are going to have a bad week or an emergency.

The second option I would use is 50-10-10-10-10-10. I know this seems more complicated or like you are going to need more money, but you won't. It really breaks down to the same thing. It is just broken down into a few more categories. The way it works is 50% of your money should go toward living expenses. When I say living expenses I mean necessities. The things on your budget that you cannot live without like food, shelter, utilities, transportation and clothing.

The first 10% should go toward giving. You should be prepared to give back to the world. You have received blessings great and small and you should return them to the universe so that you can continue to receive favor and so that other people will receive blessings too. This 10% can be your tithes if you go to church or it can be your gift fund; whatever you and your God choose. The most important thing is that you give with an open heart. I have people in my world that ask for money constantly. At one point in my life, I use to take from my savings or my living expenses until I realized that I was hurting myself to help someone else. That did not seem like the smart thing to do so I stopped doing that and set up a gift fund and that would take care of charity, tithes and gifts. Whatever was in that account was what we had to use. If someone needed $500 but there was only $300 in the account, I would tell them I can help out with $300.

The next 10% is for saving. Saving is extremely important because you will always need more money in the future for something. Whether it is to put a new roof on the house or to take a vacation, it is good to have a savings account. This way you have the money to help with emergencies, unexpected expenses or to spoil yourself a little. You should save 10% whether you are employed or self-employed. If you are self-employed, when you deposit your money, immediately transfer 10% of it to your savings account. This way you are not tempted to spend it. Having a separate savings account makes it easier for you to keep all your categories clear. Savings is not for long term; it is short term or for a specific time frame or project. Savings will get spent at some point, but try to hold on to it as long as you can and use it for what it is allocated for.

You should also put a separate 10% of your money toward investing. You might say wait a minute, I thought I just did that. No you did not. You put money toward savings. Saving and investing are two different things. Savings, like I said earlier, is short term. Investing on the other hand, is for long term; 5, 10, 20, or 30 years from now. When you put your money in a savings account, you are lucky if you get 2% interest. What this means is, if inflation is also rising at 3%, your money is not growing. If inflation is rising faster than your money is growing eventually you will lose the time value of money. So if you are not planning to use your savings in the next 6 months to 3 years, you may want to consider putting it in an investment vehicle.

Investment money is set aside for retirement, sending your children to college, buying a bigger house, starting a business or any long term goal you have that will take a capital investment. The risk with investing is no one can really determine what the stock market is going to do. For that reason, you will see losses and gains from time to time. This is okay as long as you are averaging the return you need over your time frame. For example, if you determined you need to get an average return of 9% over the next ten years, then that is the number you should focus on. Often people get scared when they see the market drop because they forget that they were going for an average. Just because the market drops this year, it does not mean that you will not hit your average over the ten year period you projected. The closer you get to the time frame or period you need the money you are investing, the more conservative you need to be. At some point, you should even take out a portion of your investment and put it into savings so that you are able to get to it when you need it. Savings should be more liquid than investments. Investments may take time to convert into real dollars like waiting on a property to sale or stock to rise.

For some of you this is elementary and you are not sure why I just explained all of that. In fact, you are thinking that I left out a bunch of information. That is true because this book is not about investing; this book is about starting over. Many different people start over; millionaires, thousandaires and poor people. Some will be familiar with saving and investing and some will never have done either a day in their lives. This little bit of information on saving and investing is a quick fix to get you started on rethinking the way you spend. This chapter is mostly concerned with cutting costs where you can. However, it is hard for me to talk about finances without making you have a spending plan. Some income is meant to be spent today and some is for the future. That is really the point. If you can cut some costs and put some of that money you were planning to spend today towards your future spending, you will be more prepared in your journey to this new place.

There are so many investment options and this chapter cannot begin to explain them all. If you do not have a Financial Advisor it is important that you get one. Even if you only meet with them twice a year, you need someone that can assist you in your financial decision making. Make sure you understand that I am saying they are assisting you. They are not leading you. They should help you see all the options while you should make the final decision on what to do. Having a Financial Advisor is just like having a tax accountant or attorney. They can tell you the details of what each financial decision will mean. They can help you see the pit falls that will come in the future. Most importantly, they can help you sift through all the information that is out there to determine what pertains to you and your situation.

Sticking with my method of budgeting, I will move on to where the next 10% should go; education. Your education savings can include college, saving for the future or current classes you or your family wants to attend. Allot 10% for education expenses so that you and your family can continue to grow and learn. You may want to take a cooking class, carpentry class or your child may want to take gymnastics. This part of your income should go to expenses like that. Plan out the activities so that you are sure you have enough money for all the things you and your family want to do.

People often forget to budget in these kinds of expenses. They usually sign up for classes and sessions on impulse. You should shop around for classes the same way you do for shoes and clothes. Find out if there is anywhere the class is offered for free, especially when there are children involved. Let them take a free class first to see if they like the sport or activity. That way if they do not like it, you do not feel bad because you did not pay for it. Try this a few times until they find something they like. Once it is clear what they enjoy, you can start paying for it.

The same is true for adults. You may be bored and just want to find something to do after your divorce or while you are looking for a new job. Take some free classes. Most of the time when we are bored, we find ways to spend money we do not have but this is counterproductive. When you do not have as much money coming in as you use to you need to really budget and plan your purchases. There is nothing wrong with getting something for free. I know the saying is you get what you pay for, but they also say the best things in life are free. So either way, focus on what you need and get that for as little money as possible. If there is something that you really want make it a reward when you accomplish something or get a bonus or when you receive an extra blessing.

The last 10% is the most important 10% and that is entertainment. This includes movies, dinners, concerts and parties. If your birthday is coming up and you want to have a party, make sure you are saving up enough money to pay for it. Your birthday is not going to be happy if you find out that you cannot eat for a week because you partied too hard (we will call that the birthday diet). Entertaining yourself is important so be sure to work it into your budget. You want to enjoy life as much as you can. Just remember what is most important and do those things first. If you are in high debt you need to take most of your entertainment money and even some of your education money and pay down that debt. When you hit a bench mark, reward yourself. Do something fun and exciting. Debt rises and if you are saving at 3% and your interest payments are 23%, you are better off paying your debt down because there is no entertainment worth the stress of high debt payments. Save your money, pay down debt and enjoy your life in the right order.

The 50-10-10-10-10-10 method is easy if you know how to live below your means. These methods will be difficult if you are living check-to-check or if you do not budget at all. Spending without budgeting can be a stressful life if you are not independently wealthy. If you are living off of the interest of your interest or if your grandparents have set you up with an endless trust fund then pay no attention to a budget. Do what you do. However, for the 95% of us whose last names are unknown, even at the lowliest of country clubs, please use a budget so that life can be more enjoyable.

Many people think that using a budget is stressful. I will bet you that if you use a budget correctly for 6 months straight you will not only have less stress but you will find that you have more money. No kidding. No late fees, no over-draft fees and you will know when your money is coming in and how it comes in so that you can plan your spending. When you plan your purchases around your income, you feel less stressed because you know what time of the month you have more money and what time you have less.

The last way you can break down your spending plan is my favorite. It is called the 4, 3, 2, 1 method. This one will keep you in line very easily if you follow it. It is good for self employed people too. Once you take out money for taxes you can begin splitting up your money in this manner. Your household expenses should be 40% of your earnings. The next 30% should go to meals, entertainment, rewards, shopping, travel and things of that nature. You should save and invest 20% of your money and the last 10% should go to gifts, tithes and charity.

For example, if your household income is $6,000 per month estimate your taxation at about $1,800. This will leave you with $4,200; 40% of that is $1,680. That should go towards things like mortgage, utilities, household maintenance and insurance. 30% of $4,200 is $1,260 and this amount should fund your dates, girl's nights out, your basketball league, amusement parks and eating out. 20% of $4,200 is $840 and that should be split up between your savings and investment accounts. The last 10%

is $420 and that should be used to pay your tithes or if you don't go to church often, use it as a gift and charity fund. People will ask to borrow money, but do not loan it to them. Just give them a gift and do not worry about getting it back. It will come back to you 100 fold.

In order to do this you may need to live in a smaller house, drive a less expensive car and curb your shopping enthusiasm. I am not suggesting you stress yourself out being frugal or stretching every dollar, I am just saying do not worry about whether you look wealthy. If you have a fancy car or big house it doesn't mean you are wealthy, it means you have a lot of bills. And if your bills exceed the amount of money you have allocated to pay then you are broke in your fancy house. Don't be careless. Spend 20-30 minutes a day managing your money and earnings and you will feel wealthy, look wealthy and actually be wealthy.

A great way to cut cost is to barter or trade. Many years ago, bartering was the only way to purchase something. Bartering is when you swap goods or services with someone instead of paying cash. For example, if you are a clothing designer and your neighbor is a printer, you would trade a shirt or dress for a set of business cards or flyers. I really like bartering for business owners because you can also use it as a form of advertising. Let's say someone walks into the printing shop and they compliment the owner on the shirt you made. The Printer can say I got it from the store next door. For an individual, you may barter on things you need like babysitting, food or landscaping. Say for instance the neighbor has a kid near the age of your kid. They want to go on a trip without the kid. Tell them you will do it if they will buy groceries for the week. If you own a lawn mower and your neighbor owns a snow blower you can use each other's tools. Be careful with this though because people tend to get possessive when it comes to tools. Be creative and find ways to barter and trade. It is okay if it feels like you are negotiating with your friends. . Once you agree on a strategy, it becomes so second nature that it is fun. Be communicative and if you think you are being used, pull back a little or ask for more. You should also make sure you are not over asking without offering.

Cutting costs can also mean partnering with someone so that you can get a better price. If you are part of a home owners association or a condo association and you know that many of the people buy from the same stores, you can negotiate some kind of discount for your organization. What if everyone in your building could get 10% off if they shopped at a certain store? That would be a great deal. You can also partner with a neighbor to buy in bulk and split it up. This is good for single people. If you and a friend or neighbor could share in the cost of the 24 pack of toilet tissue or 100 slices of cheese or 50 batteries, you all could save big. There are many ideas and several books about saving money. You can buy one if that is an area that means a lot to you or you can check the resources list at www.kinecorder.com/resources for more ideas.

When you cut costs you put yourself in a position to have more money. There are things that you will need that you may not be able to negotiate or cut cost on. For those, pay what you have to. For all other things negotiate, shop around, be patient or trade. You never know what you will find when you take the time to plan your purchases rather than buying on impulse.

I want you to get good at cutting costs so as you are starting over you can prepare for a cut in your income or spending money on your new life. If you are prepared to cut costs and you have put some of these things in place, it will free up money to do the things that will truly make you happy. If you find that you can cut cost without feeling insecure, you are really beginning to get it. Living inside your means can be difficult if you are used to spending every dollar you make and borrowing to keep up your lifestyle. In order to reduce stress, you should find it inside yourself to put some of these ideas into action.

I like processes that cut out steps so I am a big fan of automatic bill pay because you can pay your bills without having write out checks and take them to the mail box. Now, you have two options when it comes to automatic bill pay. You can set it up yourself using your bank or you can let the payee pull it out of your account at a date that they set. I choose to set it up myself using my online banking. Another reason I like automatic bill pay is, no matter where I am I know that my bills are being paid on time and I do not have to worry. By using my bank, I am in control of adjusting the day I pay a bill. Using this system will allow you to cut down on late fees, missed payments and free yourself of overdraft fees. Automatic bill pay allows you to track your spending and stay on top of your expenses.

Have direct deposit at your job or make daily deposits from your business income, so you know the money is in there to pay your bills. If you have lost your job or your business is not doing well, then cutting cost is essential and auto bill pay may be difficult but try it as much as you can. We will talk more about what to do when you do not make enough money in the next chapter.

You do not have to commit to this for life but just try it and if it is really difficult, ask for help. I am sure there are many people around you who have had your same problem. Find out what they did to get through it and talk to them about some of the things they do to save money. Saving money gives you one more thing to celebrate because there is nothing like finding a good deal.

As you see yourself saving money, start to calculate items you used to over pay for or items you used to buy and never use. Keep a list either on paper or in your head. If you stop buying something, figure out how much money you used to spend on that item and spend that money wisely or use it to put toward your debt, savings or investing. Get everyone in the house involved. Make it a game if you think that will work. Give out points and rewards and discuss why you are doing it.

When you do this you will be proud of yourself. You will begin to tell your friends and family and they will begin to put these principles into action. When that happens everyone will forget about the Joneses and begin living in real life. We have to be more financially responsible. We have to stop letting how much money we spend define our worth. If you find a way to earn millions of dollars you do not have to spend it all to feel proud of yourself. When you spend your money, do so in a manner that makes sense for your life knowing you are helping yourself grow. I am certain that as you begin to cut costs both big and small, you will see the worth in this exercise and see the worth in yourself. You are enough. You do not need to buy your friends. You do not need to keep up with your friends' purchases and you do not need a label to define who you are. You are great and powerful. Take control over your life and finances and control the next phase of your life with good spending habits. Starting over here will change some of the other areas of your life. When you have proven that you have gained control over your spending treat yourself and celebrate like a rock star.

Call to action:
1. Make a budget that you can stick to. Download mine if you do not have one.
2. Use the budget for at least 3 months

3. Find places where you can cut your costs and expenses.
4. Decide which financial planning option is right for you and begin using it in your life.
5. Find a Financial Advisor who you can work with successfully
6. Think of ways you can barter, trade or partner in order to cut costs.

Day 26 – Get Paid

Getting paid is about charging what you are worth, having different payment options, finding multiple streams of income and receiving your blessings. When you are a business owner you cannot give your product or service away for free or even price it too low because you will go out of business. When you work for someone else you have to know what your salary range should be and request the highest amount to match the work you put out. Finding ways to make money when you are not actively working is the best way to get paid. I have talked about it before but you want to be open to whatever the universe has for you plus more. When you open your heart, mind, and soul enough to do the work money begins to flow into your life. Think of creative income streams and when you see the fruit of your labor smile and say thank you.

Do you sometimes get your check at the end of the week and wonder why you went to work each day? Have you ever found out someone in the same position or a lower position makes more money than you do? When you were calculating your bills and cutting costs, did you think about your income and how you could increase it in order to live the way you want to? You have to earn more money than you spend. The first thing you have to figure out is how to earn more money. You may already know how. You may have figured it out while reading this book or you may be ready to give it some thought now.

If you did the budget, you listed all your income streams. Take a look at that list and think about how important those dollars and cents are to your survival and your bigger dream. Do you get scared when you think about your income? Do you get nervous and anxious because you want so much more but do not know how to get it? Do you get happy because you earn the money you need to earn to have the life you want, but you just have not figured out how to balance life and work? Do you get angry because you feel you work hard and have nothing to show for it? What do you feel when you look at your income and your bank account? If you share that income and bank account with someone else, how long has it been since you all have had a conversation, non argumentative, about the goals of your accounts and your income?

Money has a way of making us more *than* what we really are or in some cases more *of* what we really are. If you are selfish and you get more money you will become more selfish. If you are giving and you get more money you will become more giving. If not having enough money was always your fear and it made you very cheap, when you get more money you will only get cheaper because now you have more to keep. So whoever you are as your money grows is who you will be.

I have never believed that money was the root of all evil. I do believe that the lack of money can make you do some evil things or chasing money can make you do evil things, but money is not evil. The person who is doing the evil deed already had it in them to be evil. Money just brought it out of them. The statement "get paid" is not about taking more than your fair share. It is not about being unfair or greedy or careless. It is about making sure you are looking out for you and that you are putting systems in place that allow you to get money in every ethical way you can.

If you own a business, you should have several ways to get paid. I mean you should have several products and services but you should also have several payment methods for your customers. Some ways are put in place to make it easier for people to spend money with you. Many businesses do not take personal checks because customers write checks that their bank accounts will not cover. Now if you want to take checks, there are ways of clearing those checks and making sure the money is in the account before you accept it. You also have the option of accepting credit cards. This is another method that makes it easier for your customers to pay you. There is a mobile credit card options now so if you travel to different locations you can still get paid. This goes back to our technology lesson. If you have a business or hobby that generates income for you, make sure you are making it easy for your clients to pay you so that it is easy for you to get paid.

If you have a job or you are a consultant, make sure you have systems in place that allow you to get your money quickly and easily. Sign up for direct deposit and you will have your money before you wake up on Friday morning. Find out if this is an option for you. If you are unemployed, you can have your unemployment benefits direct deposited or put onto a debit card. If you are running a business you can have a personal account at the same bank you hold your business account and have an automatic transfer move the money into your personal account as frequently as you like. The key is getting paid and getting paid quickly.

Getting paid may seem to be difficult if you are on a fixed income like government assistance, unemployment, alimony or if your business is not making money. When this happens it is time for you to get creative. Are you employing too many people in your business? Do you need to restructure? Do you have too many expenses? Do you have enough systems in place that help you get your money from your customers, quickly? Are there other income streams you have not considered? Do you or your business have another product you could sell or cut out that would free up more money? If you have a hobby that could generate income are you utilizing it to the fullest? Are there items in your house that you do not use that you could sale? Where is the hidden money around you?

If getting paid is not really that important to you and all you need is love or all you need is the shirt on your back to feel happy, then please disregard my suggestion. However, if there are things that you like and things that you like to do that cost money, then getting paid is important. You just need to figure out your number. What amount of money would be enough? Now I am not saying you would not make more money if you could. I am saying if you never made any more money than that number, you would feel good. If you are technical, yes I am factoring in an increase for inflation so do not worry about that. If you go back to your list of the things you like and the bucket list and calculate how much you would need to fulfill your needs and wants this is the number. Add up all the things you like to do on a weekly, monthly and annual basis. Then figure out about how much money that would take and write it down here.

I would be happy earning $\underline{\hspace{3cm}}$ every $\underline{\hspace{3cm}}$.
You may be thinking of a number you need to make weekly or monthly or annually. It is your number so make it fit into your lifestyle exactly the way you imagine it. Is your number $100,000, $500,000 or is it $10,000,000? What amount of money do you think would make you feel peaceful, safe and happy? How far away are you from that number now? Do you see it as a number you can really reach? Think big and believe in yourself whether you have a job, own a business or both. When I look back at the time when I did not have enough money to live the life I desired, I found the problem was either, I did not know how much I was worth, I did not price my product or service correctly, I did not ask for the money I deserved, or I did not know how to earn money doing what I wanted to do. Sometimes all you need is a little direction and you can find the money you are looking for.

In the beginning of this book, you made a list of people you owe money to and people who owe you money. Have you paid anyone back? Have you collected any money from your debtors? Revisit that list. Who owes you money, are you going after these dollars? You may have two lists, people who owe you personally and people who owe you professionally. Have you written this money off or do you plan to get your repayment? Getting your repayment is one way to add to your income. Also, paying back money you owe someone starts the flow of energy back to you. Stop blocking your blessings by telling the universe you do not respect loan repayments. If you are giving money from your gift fund and you do not expect it back then let it go. Do not hold on to it mentally or emotionally. That money will return to you later a hundred fold. If you want your money back from the person you gave it to, the first step is to ask for it. Second, give them payment options. The third step is to understand their situation and if you know they are never going to pay you back let it go. Do not stress yourself out about it. Find other ways for them to make up that money. Maybe there are chores they can help you with. Be creative.

If you are working a job there are several ways you can add to your income. You could apply for a higher position, you could ask for a raise, you could go to a different company or you could get a second job. If you get a second job, just make sure that you really enjoy it and you are not going to want to leave, or else you are going to forget the reason you ever got a second job anyway and quit. Do something that you always wanted to do, something that brings you joy or maybe a discount on something you like. If you ask for a raise, make sure that you are on point. Make sure you have been coming to work on time, doing your assigned job and maybe even going over and beyond. Document your achievements and make sure that when it is time for a review, you are scoring high. If you are going to go for that promotion than you need to make sure you are doing all the things we just talked about and learning the job you are pursuing. Find out how to make the position more efficient and let them know your ideas when you are being interviewed. Do not tell them how only tell them what. Let them know for example, you have a system that could make accounting run smoothly. It will only cost a small investment but it will save thousands over the long run. That shows you are looking out for the company and that you plan to be there for the long run. If you are planning to change companies, make sure you are learning as much as you can to bring value to the new company. When you start to apply, make sure you are looking for positions that will allow you to grow and that allow you to use your strengths. You know what they are so identify positions that play up your strengths.

If you are on unemployment or receiving alimony and you have always wanted to start your own business, here is a chance to do it while you have some income and probably some free time. Some people are unemployable. You see things your way and you do it your way. You do not understand rules and you work the way you want to; not the way someone tells you to. Keep in mind however, there are always going to be rules. You may set some for yourself, your customers may have demands of you, or your employees may have expectations of you. It is hard to get away from rules, but being self-employed is one way to make the rules work a little bit more in your favor.

You have a list of things you like, your bucket list and you already went through the exercise that describes your life purpose. Take some time to search your soul to find out if now is a good time to pursue your life's purpose. Do you have the capital, resources and wherewithal it will take to make it happen? Did you train, take your mark, and get set so now it is time to go? Having your own business may be just the thing to help you get paid; the thing you need to help you get your life right this time. Many people start businesses; some of them succeed and some of them fail. But so what? At least they tried. Some of those people end up starting more than one business and they learn from the mistakes they made in the previous business. Being in business is tricky. There are a lot of variables, risks and rewards. Think of all of them when you are making your plan.

You know in your heart if it really is time for you to raise your prices, ask for a raise or get a second job. It is just a matter of if you are afraid of what could happen. Do not be afraid. Getting paid may be a matter of you being powerful enough to just go for it. You just might get that raise, you may get that new position and your customers may understand why you are raising your prices. Someone is getting a raise right now, someone is getting a new position right now, someone is opening the doors to their new business right now and someone is getting more for their product or service right now. It could be you. All you have to do is have a good reason, supporting documents, confidence in what you are requesting, and you will get it.

When you know how valuable you are you will get paid. Ask and you shall receive remember. If you do not receive keep asking. Have a childlike heart and spirit; ask until your heart is content. Like a child be not afraid. Like a child believe it is yours and you deserve it. Like a child you should celebrate when you get it.

Call to action:
1. Pay back loans and begin asking the people that owe you to repay.
2. Make a list of ways you can add income or raise your income.
3. One by one start to generate the new income streams you listed.
4. What amount of money would allow you to really live? Find your number and write it down.
5. Celebrate when you have achieved the new income level you desire.

Day 27 – Transferring Risk

In the financial world, transferring risk usually applies to using other people's money or insurance. That is a big part of what this chapter is about. The other part is about making sure you have calculated the risk you are taking and determine if you have to do it.

I will start this chapter with the discussion transferring risk to someone who can do it with less risk. What that means is there are many things that you can do but just because you can, does not mean you should. You could represent yourself in a court case or you could find an attorney more capable who can try the case for you. The attorney has studied the law and the risk of you losing is greater if you take the case on your own. Hiring a smart, capable attorney is the best way to transfer the risk in this situation. Another examples would be taxes. You may have taxes that are more complicated than normal. You could file your taxes yourself and risk the IRS auditing you later or you could call a capable accountant who knows this year's tax laws and can therefore help you file properly and get the money back you have coming to you.

In cases like both of these this is a matter of trust. You have to trust your attorney or your accountant. Many times if you have been burned once you will vow to never get assistance again. Every attorney, accountant, hairstylist, babysitter or doctor is bad. If you had a bad experience with one you may want to look at your interview process. Be thorough, do your research and ask for referrals.

Asking for a referral is a good way to find someone you can trust. Ask other people what their experience was like and make an informed decision. Do your research and find the one that can work the way you expect them to. There will be red flags that will indicate if someone is not good at what they do. Pay attention to them and address them accordingly. Also, decide what things you can put up with or compromise on. If you have an attorney who knows the law and how to make it work in your favor but she is not good at returning phone calls, decide which one is more important. Are you okay with calling a few times before you get through or talking to an assistant, or do you need to talk with your attorney every time you get the need? If that is the case, then you may want to do the research and find someone who is good at returning calls and the knowledge they bring may be secondary to you. You may have to trade off in some areas but you decide what areas you can trade.

Transferring the risk is about putting things in place that will allow you to be your best even if it does cost you. Do not cut costs when it comes to paying for things that you cannot successfully do yourself. If you like quality work, hire a quality technician. If you run the risk of setting your house on fire, blowing your car up or causing more damage than you fixed, just hire the right person.

Transferring the risk can also apply to using other people's money. When you purchase a house you are not thinking of coming up with the entire purchase amount. You are saving up a down payment and you will get a mortgage loan for the rest. This is a form of transferring the risk. You are going into business with the mortgage company. You are asking them to front you the money until you are able to pay them back. Your goal if you plan to live there forever should be to pay them back as quickly as possible so that you pay less interest. There is a cost to transferring the risk however; an accelerated payment plan is a way to minimize that cost. If you have a short term goal for the property and you plan to sell it in the next 5-7 years, then you may not want to accelerate the payments. You may want an interest only loan or you may want to pay as little as possible so that you keep as much of your money in your pocket now. When you sell the property you can give the bank their capital back and you keep the profit. This is not only transferring the risk, this is also getting paid. You are doing great!

If you are starting a business you may want investors to help you with the start-up capital you need to run the business. You pay them back when the business makes a profit. You put in the sweat equity and run the business and they put up the monetary equity to fund the business. In this case, transferring the risk can be a win-win situation if the business is successful. The investor gets their money back plus interest and you get to continue to run your company.

The most common way to transfer risk is with insurance. I will admit that transferring the risk when it comes to insurance can be tricky. Unlike that win-win situation we talked about when transferring the risk in a successful business, insurance is usually not a win-win situation. Someone is going to lose some money. When it comes to auto insurance, if you are successful in never having a car accident or having to file a claim, then you lose because you paid in premiums that you will not ever get back. When you have an accident the company allows you to pay a small amount, your deductible, and they pay the rest. If there was a lot of damage done this situation worked in your favor. There are times when insurance can help. The objective of the insurance company is not to pay a claim. So they have exclusions and limitations that legally allow them to get out of it. Make sure you speak with your insurance agent to ensure you have all your bases covered, pay your premiums and do what you are supposed to. When you file a claim and the insurance company has to pay, then you have successfully transferred the risk to them.

Let's use life insurance for our example. You have a term life insurance policy that says if you die within the 20 years that you own the policy, we will give your family $1,000,000. Let's say you owned the policy for 18 years and died. You paid your premiums to the insurance company and for this examples let's say they added up to $20,000. Now they have to give your family $1,000,000. That is a great transfer of risk if you can keep up the insurance payments long enough, your family can have a gift from you that can help them live the life you always dreamed of them living.

There are many ways to transfer risk. From asking someone more capable of doing something to do it for you, to buying insurance to cover something you cannot afford to replace, to using someone else's money to fund a project you do not have the assets to produce. Have you thought about ways you have already transferred risk and are there other ways you can transfer risk?

Make a list of some of the ways you have already transferred risk.

_____

_____

_____

_____

_____

_____

_____

_____

Make a list of new ways you can transfer risk that will allow you to get to the next level or to protect something you cannot afford to reproduce or lose.

_____

_____

_____

_____

_____

_____

_____

_____

Call to action:
1. Review all your insurance policies and make sure they are right for your situation.
2. Make a list of things you need to protect or ways you can transfer risk.
3. Start putting those things in place.

Day 28 – Leaving a Legacy

We just finished talking about transferring risk and how life insurance can help you do that. Life insurance can also help you leave a legacy. Now you do not want to have more insurance than you need but you do not want to end up with less either. Make sure you have enough life insurance to pay off your expenses including debts and funeral costs. If you have 4 children that you want to send to college, you need to have enough insurance today to take care of those four children and anyone else who is relying on your income. You have to plan for the worst and be prepared to give your loved ones what you would give them if you were alive.

It is my dream that the next generation and the generations to follow will not have to struggle. They will have a nest egg or inheritance that will afford them a full life. I will also leave them educational tools that will teach them how to use their money wisely and to pass down to other generations more than what they had so the legacy can continue. Leaving a legacy is about more than just leaving money to your children or grandchildren. Leaving a legacy is about leaving money, a sense of pride, enough knowledge and a memory. Leaving a legacy is like leaving a blue print to say this is how you do what I did. Martin Luther King Jr. left a legacy for future generations. He and his generation suffered so the next generations would not have to. He showed us how to get things done in this country, how to sacrifice and how to excel.

Maybe your grandparents taught you by their work ethic. Maybe your neighbors taught you when you were growing up by using the, "it takes a village to raise a child" mentality. Think of all the legacies that were left for you. Write down where you have benefited from other people's struggle, hard work or forward thinking. You can name personal legacies or general legacies like the civil rights movement.

_____

_____

_____

_____

_____

_____

_____

_____

_____

_____

_____

_____

_____

How have these legacies helped you? Were you able to get jobs because of programs that were in place or relationships your parents built? Were you able to get an education because of someone else's fight or from an education fund your grandparents set up? Did you have an example of life insurance working in your life or the life of someone you know? Write a paragraph about how the things you listed above have affected your life.

_____

_____

_____

_____

_____

_____

_____

_____

_____

_____

_____

_____

Did writing this paragraph help you think about legacies you would like to continue or start? Maybe you have children or grandchildren and you want to see them live the life you were never able to live. Do you have things you want to teach to the next generation? Do you have enough life insurance to allow your family to go on without struggling? Write down what kind of legacy you would like to leave.

_____

_____

_____

_____

_____

_____

_____

_____

_____

_____

_____

_____

_____

_____

_____

_____

I want you to take the next step and actually write out a Will. It will not be a legal document; you are still going to need to see an estate planning attorney, but by the time you go to the attorney you will know what you want to leave and how you want to leave it. You will just need the attorney to tell you the best way to reach your goals. Write a Will and include all the things you have that you want to pass down. If there is something you want to pass down like stories, put that in there too. You can write your stories down or video tape them or start inviting your family over and sharing the stories.

Leave everything you can think of to the people or person you think will benefit from it the most. Write from your heart. What does your heart and soul want to leave your family and the world? How do you want to be remembered? What do you have that you can pass down to generations to come? Write your Will and be as generous as you like. You can even leave things that you do not have yet. Leave as much as you want to whomever you want. Make the world a better place with all the things you leave behind. What is your last Will and Testament?

_____
_____
_____
_____
_____
_____
_____
_____
_____
_____
_____
_____
_____
_____
_____
_____
_____
_____
_____
_____
_____
_____
_____
_____
_____
_____
_____
_____
_____

How do you feel about the life you have lead and the stories you have left behind? When people see your journey will they be inspired? There are people in the world who are watching you, who are looking up to you and who are counting on you. Do your part to make the world, especially your world, a better place. When you put these things in place you will have changed the world. Somebody's world will be different because you lived.

Call to action:
1. List legacies that you have benefited from.
2. Write a paragraph describing how you have benefited
3. Make a list of legacies you would like to leave.

Day 29 – Making Good Decisions

I could write an entire book on this subject, but for now I will sum up what I know in to this chapter. I am going to tell you a story and I will give you a chance to write down how you would have handled the situation and why you would have handled it this way. I will give you a hint up front on how to make good decisions. There are a few things I do to make sure I am making the best decision. The first thing I do is ask myself a series of questions. Second, I go to someone whose advice I trust, and third I think fast but react slow. Thinking things through is usually the best way to avoid making mistakes. There are a few questions I ask myself before I make a decision. I normally mentally answer them and based on my answers I decide whether or not I should do it. You can write your answers down if that helps you.

What are all my options?

Where is this decision likely to lead me?

Am I following the crowd?

Can I handle the consequences if things do not turn out the way I planned?

Is there a better way?

Can I do this and should I do this?

Asking for advice can be helpful if you have someone you trust and respect to give you all the facts and help you answer some of those questions above that you may not know the answers to. If you cannot think of anyone you trust and respect, you may need to go to the list of resources to help. Many times when we are under pressure we cannot think straight. That is why we go through these exercises so that when you are in the middle of a crisis you do not have to think. For some people asking for advice may mean going into prayer and asking God to give them direction. You may have put God on your resource page. It is okay to trust more than one person and get advice from different angles. However, do not confuse yourself by asking too many people's opinion. Ask someone wise and then take that advice and make your own decision.

At the end of this story I want you to write down how you would have handled the situation. You can use the above method or you can use the method you normally use to make decisions. There is no right or wrong answers. This is an exercise for you to practice asking yourself the questions and for you to evaluate your current decision making skills.

Trisha owns a clothing store on Melrose Avenue in Los Angeles. She opened the store three years ago but has been working in retail fashion since she was in high school. She carries only 5 clothing lines in the store and one of them is her own. She also sells one brand of shoes and a few accessories. Trisha loves her business but is often stressed out about the pressure she has to take on as a business owner and new wife. Most of Trisha's friends feel that she is successful because she is her own boss and she loves what she does. Every night Trisha brings homework from the store; bills that need to be paid, decisions that need to get made and repairs that have to get mended on her clothing. The store closes at 7:00 most days, except on Saturday she closes at 9:00 so she can catch those last minute shoppers who need a new outfit to go out.

Four years ago Trisha met Bruce and they got married last summer. Bruce is a cameraman by day and guitar player on the weekends with his band. He loves his life because he gets to do what most people dream about. Trisha and Bruce never get to spend time together. He says it is because she is always working and she says it is because he is always with his friends. One day Bruce and his friends enter a contest to win a trip and Bruce won. He had the choice to bring anyone he wanted on the trip with him.

He could bring one of his friends or he could bring his wife. He would be happy either way but he wished that they all could go.

When Trisha and Bruce got home that evening they began to talk and an argument started to brew. Trisha wanted to know why Bruce could not come by the store and help her close up and he wanted to know why she could not close up early before she got tired and hang out with their friends. She was the boss and she made the decisions so why not just close at 6:00? Trisha hated when Bruce would try to run her business. She chose that time for a reason and she was not going to change it now because her customers were used to it.

Before the argument got too bad, they both went in separate rooms to stay out of each other's way. They had had this same argument a hundred times and it always ended up the same way. Trisha continues to pay more attention to her business than she does to her husband. She will not close earlier and she will not hire someone else to help her. Bruce always chooses to hang out with his friends, practice their set, or go out to eat. He does not go to the store to help Trisha close because she will not listen to him and close early.

While Trisha was cleaning up, she found Bruce's pants on the floor where he always leaves them. She picks up the jeans, pulls the stuff out of his pockets, puts it on his night stand and throws the jeans in the laundry like she always does. Before walking away, she sees what looks like a boarding pass. What is that, she asked herself? She had to know. She picked it up and read it and saw that Bruce had won a trip. She was surprised that he did not tell her about it and wondering if he was going to. She also noticed that the trip dates were the same as a big tradeshow she attends every year for her business. She was angry but she was also hurt. What happened to the days when he used to call her as soon as something good happened to him? Trisha wanted to ask him about it but she also wanted to see how he was going to handle it. Now, she did not know what she would do about the trade show. She could not miss it because she always gets good business there. She got the jeans out of the laundry basket, put the stuff back in his pocket and put them right back on the floor. She did not want to talk to him tonight so she got in the bed and went to sleep.

Bruce kept thinking about the trip he had won and who he was going to take. He and Trisha never really went on their honeymoon because they were both working so much, but a fun trip with his buddy would be right on-time. He could not believe that he was even hesitating. In the past he would have called Trisha immediately and told her to get her bikini ready. Now he feared she would find a way to say no.

Two weeks went past and they kept their same daily routine; Bruce and his friends, Trisha and her store. Then Sunday came. Sunday was their day to hang out. Trisha closed the store at 5:00 on Sundays so they always went to dinner at their favorite place or some new place they heard about. Dinner started out quiet. Neither of them seemed to have much to talk about. Deep down inside, they both had so much to say but did not know where to begin. Trisha wanted to ask him about the trip but she knew she would have to then choose between him and the trade show. She missed talking to him and she had so many things she wanted to tell him about the business but she knew he would try to tell her what to do and she did not want advice. Bruce wanted to tell Trisha about the trip but he knew he would have to choose between her and his best friend. He wanted to ask her about the store but whenever he did she always got defensive and never let him be a part of anything dealing with it. That's why he could not understand why she wanted him to come by. She never let him help anyway. The waiter came by and said, "Is everything okay?" They looked at each other and answered, "Yes, we're fine." That was not the truth. Everything was not okay. They were not fine. They really needed to talk and make some major decisions.

If you were Trisha how would you handle this? If you were Bruce how would you handle it? Remember, you do not know what the other one is thinking so do not answer based on the information I gave you. Answer based on the information you would have if you were that person. Would you go on the trip with your friend, pretending like he won it and not tell your wife that she could have been an option? Would you never bring it up to your husband and just go on your business trip? Would you express your stress about your clothing store? Would you try to be a part of your wife's business? Answer these questions and any questions you think need to be answered. Read over the story again if necessary to ensure you have all the information you need to make your decisions.

Make a decision for Bruce.

_____
_____
_____
_____
_____
_____
_____
_____

Make a decision for Trisha.

_____
_____
_____
_____
_____
_____
_____
_____

Now that you have made your decision, is this the way you normally make decisions? Do you think the decision you made for Trisha will lead to the life she wants? Do you think the decision you made for Bruce will lead to the life he wants? What decisions in your life do you need to address? What will lead you to where you want to be?

Call to action:
1. Make a decision for Bruce.
2. Make a decision for Trisha.
3. Make a list of decisions that you need to make.
4. Start by asking yourself the decision making questions then make a firm decision.

Day 30 – Reward Yourself

I am so proud of you for making it this far in the program. You have worked through some of your challenges. You have changed your way of thinking. You have made some milestones, hit benchmarks, set goals and accomplished some of them already I am sure. And the biggest achievement of all is that you did not stop. There were some reflections and changes you had to make that could have made you say forget it. But you sacrificed, went through the discomfort, and made it through to the other side.

_____

_____

_____

_____

_____

_____

_____

_____

_____

_____

_____

There is no formal graduation ceremony set-up but we are going to celebrate anyway. Take something from your "things I like list" or your "bucket list" and do it big. Pick something you know will make you happier than ever. Bring someone with you and tell them about the life changing work you have done, share your accomplishment, and have a good time. Tomorrow, read the last chapter and remember two things: 1) you can start over whenever you like and as often as you like and 2) life is not about the breaths we take every moment, but about the moments that take our breath away. So live a breathtaking life.

Call to action:

1. Write down your reflection on the work you have done with this book in the space above.
2. Email a message with your testimony to kc@kinecorder.com
3. Tell someone about the changes you made in the last few weeks and how you did it.

Day 1 – Do the work

Please understand that after 30 days a fairy godmother is not going to appear and wave her magic wand and make your life different. This chapter is called "Do the work" because this is when it all begins. This is when you apply all the principles we talked about in each chapter and when you go back and refresh yourself on the principles that you needed more time on. This is the point when you stop thinking and put some actions behind your thoughts; this is "go."

You may have already noticed some changes happening in your life. Take the time now to acknowledge those changes if you have not already. Thank yourself for doing what you were supposed to do. Thank the change for happening. If it was money, say thank you for the additional income. If it was a job or business opportunity, say thank you. Write down one of those events now. No matter how big or small, pick one and write it down. Tell how you saw the principles working in your life. Express how life will be with this new blessing. Talk about how you will use what you learned again and again and again. Explain how starting over is going to finally help you get the life you desire.

_____

_____

_____

_____

_____

_____

_____

_____

_____

_____

_____

_____

_____

_____

_____

_____

_____

_____

_____

_____

_____

_____

_____

_____

_____

_____

_____

_____

_____

_____

_____

_____

From here on out you should have the "attitude of gratitude." Say thank you often to yourself, to your creator, to those who help you and to the universe for shifting in your direction. Act grateful and do not take any blessing for granted. Not everyone is where you are mentally, physically, spiritually or emotionally.

What are you going to do now? After reading most self-help books or going to seminars you are motivated now but a few days later you forget what you heard and you go back to your old ways. This book and the workshop both give you the power to recall and re-inspire yourself. You can go back to any of the exercises you learned. You can schedule on your weekly activity sheet, time to study and re-inspire yourself. Every week you are not only doing things that will allow you to accomplish your goals, but you are going to find ways to inspire and reward yourself along the way as well.

You will also share your experience from the book and your accomplishments with others around you and that will help you stay motivated. You have finished the book and that is an accomplishment so be sure to write it down. Also, find a chapter in the book that you would like to brush up on or rediscover. Write this on your activity list as something to do once a week or once a month if you have not already done so.

Run your personal and professional life with respect and dignity. You are mastering the Art of Starting Over and I am proud to have been a part of your journey. Do not stop now. Continue to pursue your happiness. Visit my website whenever you like and send emails with your updates.

This is the last motivational book you will ever need.
If you want to feel inspired, read it again or simply read what you wrote.
That is your blue print it should keep you going.

That is truly how strongly I feel about *The Art of Starting Over*, but these are just my feelings. If you have a need to read more I have some suggestions. While I would like to think that everything I needed I had inside me all my life, the truth is my ideas do not stand in isolation. I have read many spiritual, motivational and planning books. My experience, my gut feelings and these books have helped me formulate what I now call the guide to creating more peace, power and pleasure in your personal life.

The following books are my recommendations:

Secrets of a Millionaire Mind
        -T. Herv Eker
The Power of the Subconscious mind
        -Joseph Murphy, Ph.D., D.D
        -revised by Ian McMahan, Ph.D

Mentored by a Millionaire
        -Steven K. Scott

Start Where You Are
        -Chris Garner with Mim Eichler Rivas

The Rules of Money
        -Richard Templar

The Power of Nice
Linda Kaplan Thaler & Robin Koval

-Be Good, Be Happy, Be You!

- KC